I0605598

LESS IS LIBERATION

Finding Freedom from a Life of Overwhelm

LESS IS LIBERATION

CHRISTINE PLATT

New York

Balance
Hachette Book Group
1290 Avenue of the Americas
New York, NY 10104
GCP-Balance.com
@GCPBalance

First Edition: October 2025

Balance is an imprint of Grand Central Publishing. The Balance name and logo are registered trademarks of Hachette Book Group, Inc.

The publisher is not responsible for websites (or their content) that are not owned by the publisher.

The Hachette Speakers Bureau provides a wide range of authors for speaking events. To find out more, go to hachettespeakersbureau.com or email HachetteSpeakers@hbgusa.com.

Balance books may be purchased in bulk for business, educational, or promotional use. For information, please contact your local bookseller or the Hachette Book Group Special Markets Department at special.markets@hbgusa.com.

Print book interior design by Amnet ContentSource

Library of Congress Control Number: 2025939261
ISBNs: 9781538758304 (hardcover), 9781538758328 (ebook)

Printed in the United States of America

LSC-C

Printing 1, 2025

To who I was, who I am now, and

who I am becoming.

Sankofa (pronounced *SAHN*-koh-fah)

"Se wo were fi na wosankofa a yenkyi."—Ghanian proverb

"It is not wrong to go back for that which you have forgotten."

CONTENTS

Introduction 1

PART I: THE COMMITMENT

1 Understanding Our Overwhelm 15

2 The Life You're Seeking Freedom From 43

3 The Journey of Liberation 69

PART II: THE NECESSITIES

4 Assess the Wells 83

5 Heal the Wells 101

6 Protect the Wells 117

PART III: THE LIFESTYLE

7 Facets of Freedom 135

8 The Life You're Seeking Freedom For 149

9 Fill the Wells 153

Afterword 173

Acknowledgments 177

Notes 179

Index 183

Your Notes 189

About the Author 197

INTRODUCTION

As I write these words, I am sitting under a traditional Berber-style tent made of woven camel hair draped over hand-carved wooden posts overlooking the golden sands of the Sahara Desert. And I am literally *writing.* Old-school style. Inking these words onto lined pages in a leather-bound journal gifted by a dear friend to chronicle my ten-day Moroccan adventure. A journey I almost missed out on experiencing. Because, well, as you might suspect from this book's subtitle, I was concerned about being overwhelmed. Specifically, the overwhelm of traveling abroad amid a looming publishing deadline.

Bringing this journal in lieu of my laptop was a compromise. A bargaining with the ever-elusive work-life balance I have yet to fully understand or been able to achieve. There is something about the phrase leading with "work" before "life" that never sat right with me. But alas, even though I *am* on vacation, I *do* need to work. So, I promised myself that I would write by hand daily, that the words might even flow easier without the pressure of staring at a screen. And I was right, I have no regrets.

Morocco is a beautiful country, a place I have longed to visit for over a decade. I have hiked through the high Atlas Mountains and daydreamed for hours as we drove through low rosebush-filled valleys. Despite having a tailored itinerary, opportunities for reflection and restoration are plentiful. Occasionally, I wish my friends were here to share in this experience. But, mostly, I am grateful to be among strangers. Because I need this trip in so many ways and for so many reasons. To be reminded of who I am. And to sit in the discomfort of discovering who I am becoming without others' interruption or commentary, no matter how loving.

Yesterday, we arrived at our current destination in the Sahara, and it feels like such an honor to be here, like I am truly blessed. For every year that I move a bit further from the naivety of my youth, I am reminded that tomorrow is not promised. As I near my fiftieth birthday, I know this trip is a once-in-a-lifetime experience. I know that even if I am gifted another tomorrow, it will never be the same as today.

And today, I am smiling as I write these words. Proud of myself for finding a way to balance the gift of life—and choosing to enjoy and experience it—with work that I love. Smiling because there was a time, not so long ago, when instead of writing this introduction by hand against the backdrop of a bright Moroccan mid-morning sun, I would be sitting at my desk, hunched over as I glared at my laptop's backlight. There was a time, not so long ago, when I would be overwhelmed, angrily typing while silently cursing about how it seemed I was always working toward something in my life instead of living it.

I am smiling because, as I write these words, I not only feel free, but I also realize that *I am free*.

At this Saharan campsite, where modern glamping tents equipped with conveniences like rain shower heads and elegant light fixtures are arranged in neat rows, our hosts *do* provide Wi-Fi service. Yet another luxury for us foreigners who think we cannot go a day without connecting to the internet. The irony being, of course, that since we arrived yesterday, our once-tense bodies swaying in surrender to the rhythmic gait of camels slowly carrying us across the sandscape, none of us have actually connected to said Wi-Fi.

Instead, last night, after oohing and aahing at our accommodations, we returned outdoors to gaze up at the blue-black sky twinkling with seemingly thousands of stars. Instead, after a traditional Moroccan dinner of tagine-cooked dishes, we sat around a large bonfire with colorful wool blankets draped over our shoulders, talking to strangers from other countries, quickly becoming friends. All of us admitting our shared affliction of constantly going and doing . . . and how wonderful it felt to stop, if only for a short moment, to enjoy our long-overdue vacations.

We tried to remember the last time we watched a setting sun. We laughed, an embarrassed collective laughter, as we shamefully acknowledged how close we'd come to missing those twenty-six minutes of splendor. Our guides had to ~~force~~ encourage us to dismount from the camels, lay our blankets on the cooling sand, get comfortable, and *relax*. And thankfully so. For it was a sacred time that afforded us all what we needed.

Twenty-six minutes.

Such a short period of stillness, yet it felt like an eternity.

As we settled into the Sahara, the camels rested with their nomadic guides, which was a surprise because I selfishly believed and, yes, even expected, these majestic animals to continue without respite until we reached our destination. This time afforded rest for us foreigners too. For us to stop being so anxious about the desert glampsite awaiting us. To stop asking *where* exactly we were going and *when* exactly we would arrive. To instead do nothing more than take in, soak in, and bask in a surreal moment on this shared timeline in our lives.

I will never forget quietly watching the horizon in wonder. The orange sun descending upon the tips of golden-pink sand dunes. The bluest parts of the vast sky gradually progressing into a deep, dark purple. How peaceful, how beautiful, how humbling it was to just be. To just appreciate the simple, magnificent pleasure of being present and at one with nature.

I am still in awe of this dreamlike sunset that occurred less than twenty-four hours ago. I am still smiling at yet another new core memory where I not only felt free but also realized that *I am free*. Liberated from a life of constantly doing, as I learn to embrace the act of simply being.

Please know that I share these moments from my trip to Morocco not to be pretentious or boastful; rather, it is my intention to encourage you as you begin *your* journey to find freedom from overwhelm. To show you that it is possible to prioritize the gift of life—and choose to enjoy and experience it—as opposed to doing the most to the point of resentment. May each small reflection from my Moroccan adventure amid a looming publishing deadline serve as evidence that we *can* do work that we love without compromising who we are, what we want, or what we deserve.

We simply must learn to be intentional about honoring ourselves.

Less Is Liberation follows in the footsteps of *The Afrominimalist's Guide to Living with Less*, which explored the psychology, ownership, and benefits of releasing things that no longer serve us. Choosing to live with less in my home and wardrobe had not only helped me reduce my overconsumption but also served as a gateway to the practice of intentional living. As a matter of course, it made sense that my next book would address how to release the limiting beliefs that cause our limiting behaviors—the internal and external catalysts of our overwhelm. All was going well until I came up against a challenge I had not anticipated: It is incredibly difficult, and perhaps impossible, to write about personal transformation without confronting one's own personal roadblocks.

Despite my plan to keep the lessons in *Less Is Liberation* surface level, life forced me to go deep. Only now do I realize what seemed to be a series of unfortunate events was divine intervention forcing me to "do the work." From a medical diagnosis that disrupted my professional life to my empty-nester years being quite full with the sandwich generation pressures of caring for both my senior mother and college senior, and my insistence to try to manage it all and everything in between . . . until I couldn't.

Life—not research—is how I learned what happens when doing the most becomes our baseline, and we normalize living in a constant state of overwhelm. The years that I spent writing this book were also spent in self-discovery. While researching how to identify common limiting beliefs, I also learned how to assess and confront my own: people-pleasing, negative self-talk, overcommitting, over-functioning, and overachieving. The tendency to make personal sacrifices in the name of success. All of which led to me becoming self-aware of a very sobering truth: The choices I'd made in the past had finally caught up to me in the present.

Life—not research—is what led me to discover the intricate relationship between our overwhelm and overall well-being. Many of us were living in a constant state of overwhelm before the COVID-19 pandemic, and it seems nearly everyone is experiencing overwhelm trying to navigate the uncertainty of its aftermath. Our lives have been forever altered. Our new reality is a reminder that we are still in the early stages of uncovering the pandemic's lasting implications and impact on humanity. Our once familiar and, perhaps, even manageable overwhelm is now exacerbated by this fateful universal marker that seems to have forever changed our understanding of time and temperance.

We are overwhelmed as we try to establish new precedents to govern our lives and livelihoods. Overwhelmed as we try to keep working, all the while knowing we need to be healing. Overwhelmed as we try to exist and coexist amid global wars while fighting to end the battles raging with and within ourselves. Overwhelmed as we try to keep loving, to not let anticipatory grief rule our hearts now that we are ever more aware of the fragility of life.

I have rewritten these pages many times, with each revision holding a deeper understanding that we are all, in some capacity, still grappling with our respective recoveries from *that* unprecedented time. Even those of us who did not break had to bend more than we ever thought we could (or would ever have to) simply to survive. We are all trying to reclaim, redefine, and rediscover ourselves—who we once were, who we are now, and who we want to become. And although overwhelming, this unprecedented time post-pandemic is also an offering. A rare occasion that has the potential to not only be life-changing but also life-giving. A reminder that we can—we must—allow ourselves to grieve the past so that we can heal and begin the beautiful work of caring for our overall well-being now. We *can* find freedom from our lives of overwhelm.

We simply must learn to be intentional about honoring ourselves.

Life—not research—also taught me that overwhelm as a state of being is nondiscriminatory, capable of affecting anyone and everyone regardless of our age or identities. Given my own heritage and scholarship in African diasporic lived experiences, I believe it is important to highlight how overwhelm uniquely impacts people of the global majority, with a focus on Black people in America. Especially Black women.* And for one simple reason: I want us to understand the reasons why we are more prone and susceptible to doing the most.

* Please note that I use the term "Black woman" as an inclusive term to include *anyone* who identifies as a woman, including transgender women and femmes.

> "The most unprotected person in America is the Black woman. The most neglected person in America is the Black woman."—Malcolm X

Black women, we are the reason I share some of my most intimate truths—because I know firsthand the risks and harsh realities that arise when we neglect the care and keeping of ourselves. Throughout *Less Is Liberation*, you will find "Love Notes" that speak directly to the cultural and generational limiting beliefs that are often the source of our overwhelm. Each Love Note is a reminder that our choices have the power to keep us from living the lives we want and deserve, and if we are not careful, also cost us our lives.

The legacies that we inherited are often painful to acknowledge and accept, which is why doing the inner work to understand our "why" can be challenging. But if we want to be free, if we want to be well, we must (re)visit our past. We must remember our origin stories, those that we still need to hold dear because they empower and sustain us, and those that we need to let go because they are no longer applicable or were never ours to hold. We must understand that many of our ancestors' sobering anecdotes are no longer accurate and, therefore, no longer beneficial to our modern-day lives and livelihoods.

Indeed, Black women have a complicated relationship with work, wealth, and wellness, and this is largely because of what we have (and haven't) seen represented by our caregivers and communities. Many of us still believe we have to work twice as hard to be seen as half as good. Many of us *are* wealthy, among the top 5–10 percent of earners in the United States[†], but we

---

[†] As of 2024, the annual adjusted gross income (AGI) thresholds to be among the top earners in the United States are as follows: top 1 percent AGI of at least

don't know it because we still believe talking about money is taboo. Many of us fail to understand that none of this—not our titles or professional reputations nor our bank account balances—matter more than our well-being.

Regardless of our success, many of us are but one generation removed from scarcity—a fear that is often at the root of the limiting belief that we are but one choice, one wrong decision from being back to where we started. So, we say yes when we really want to say no. We choose to take on more even when we know we are at (or have surpassed) our capacity. We refuse to pause to care for ourselves, declaring "we must persist" even when we know we are *thisclose* to collapsing under the pressure.

Many Black women carry an unseen burden: that one mistake might result in us returning to the dire circumstances we experienced in childhood or worked hard to escape in adulthood. There is also an added weight: If that were to happen, it would not only impact our own lives but also have a ripple effect. Because when we are blessed with success and abundance, it is never ours alone.

Ask any Black woman and she will tell you—someone somewhere is always depending on her for something.

I do not know any Black woman—not one—who is solely responsible for herself.

Love Notes pay homage to that truth and serve as tributes that not only are Black women in dire need of less—to do, to have, and to be responsible for—we are first and foremost deserving.

$787,712; top 5 percent AGI of at least $290,185; and top 10 percent AGI of at least $169,800. Source: Aimee Picchi, "Here's How Much Money You Need to Earn to Join the Top 1% in Every U.S. State," *MoneyWatch*, CBS News, July 24, 2024.

A LOVE NOTE TO BLACK WOMEN

It Is Time to Stop Living a Life of Overwhelm

Oh, my dear sister. Not only do I see you, but I have also been right where you are, doing exactly what you are doing: living in a constant state of being unwell. Because that is what the feeling we call "overwhelm" actually is: a sign, a symptom that we have not been caring for our overall well-being. Unfortunately, we tend to miss the warning . . . until it is too late.

Black women are a unique intersectional demographic. The most likely to survive being born prematurely.[1] The most likely to pursue entrepreneurship.[2] The most likely to enroll in higher education.[3] The most likely to lead and participate in grassroots and community-centered organizations.[4] At 92 percent, we are the most likely to vote and shape political landscapes.[5]

Somehow, we embody both the regality of our African ancestors before our legacies were altered by the transatlantic slave trade . . . and the inherited expectations of our foremothers who were forced to till, toil, labor, birth, and nurture everything and everyone to prove their worth.

Somehow, it seems we are able to do it all (and look damn good doing it!).

We are highly capable. Highly competent. Highly versatile. And highly adaptable. No matter the task, we are highly dependable and will get the job done, even if it means taking on others' responsibilities in addition to our own. We do our work with confidence and grace. Our appearance is pristine. Our demeanor a reflection of the words of wisdom from the women who raised us on how to look and perform if we want to survive.

Only when we are alone or in trusted company are we able to be honest with ourselves and one another: How we look does not always align with how we feel.

We are worn and weary of everything we are expected to be and do, and everyone we are expected to fix and save. We have been of and in service to others since we were young. It seems we were born to mother—first our siblings and play cousins; then our partners, our lovers, our children, and others' children; and finally, when we are older, our parents and elders.

All the while, we neglect mothering ourselves.

Who we are is all we know. The Black women we grew up watching serve as the backbones of our families and communities and are what many of us have become: overworked and underpaid, selfless and self-sacrificing. And that has to change.

We have to change.

Feeling overwhelmed is a biological trigger, an indicator that we are unwell. But because we have spent so much of our lives surviving (and, unfortunately, believing that we are thriving) in this constant state of being, we no longer recognize when our bodies are pleading with us to pause, to take a moment. We no longer heed the warning to stop caring for everyone else and start caring for ourselves. Until, sadly, we face challenges that force us to prioritize our well-being. Until, sadly, the lifelong compounded damage to our weathered bodies, minds, and souls cannot be undone.

Being overwhelmed is costing Black women more than our livelihoods—it is costing us our lives. And that has to change.

***We* have to change.**

We simply must learn to be intentional about honoring ourselves.

Love Notes are my offering to the growing body of literature centered on educating and empowering Black women to prioritize our overall well-being. I encourage everyone to read them to become more adept at recognizing when Black women are in need of care so you know when to intervene and offer support. Because "All the women in me are tired" is more than a colloquialism—it is often a cry for help.

It is my hope that Black women read each Love Note as a psalm and receive it as a healing balm. May they also serve as reminders that many of us are blessed to be the first generation to have the awareness and resources to invest in ourselves. The decision to seek freedom from a life of overwhelm is indeed a privilege. *Our* privilege. What a gift we have been given to pursue personal liberation beyond our foremothers' wildest dreams—a life of doing less for others so we have more time to care for ourselves.

As I sit in the Sahara writing this introduction, I now know that *Less Is Liberation* is so much more than I ever imagined it would be. It is a memoir that chronicles my healing journey, and a manifesto that feels sacred. It is an invitation—your invitation—to learn how to honor yourself by making the commitment to understand the overwhelming life you are seeking freedom from so that you can enjoy the life you are seeking freedom for: where you are well. It is an opportunity to embrace less—to do, to have, to be responsible for—as a lifestyle that allows us to live *in* abundance . . . not just with abundance.

Less is both liberation and a lifestyle because it centers on what is perhaps our most underutilized superpower: being intentional with our choices.

We do not have to have so many things—we can choose less and enjoy having only what we need, use, and love.

We do not have to have so many obligations—we can choose less and be fully committed to what we truly have time for.

We do not have to have so many priorities—we can choose less and find ease in not having a never-ending to-do list.

We do not have to have so many relationships that feel transactional—we can choose less and have more genuine connections.

We do not have to do the most to the point of being unwell—we can do less and care for our ourselves: physically, mentally, emotionally, socially, and spiritually.

Finding freedom from a life of overwhelm is more than a premise. The very act of seeking freedom is personal. The work of liberation always has and always will begin with Self. We must honor our longings before we can help others get free. We must embody liberation to show others that we are here for more than a life of doing.

My friend, we are here for a life of being.

Welcome to the journey—your journey—of finding freedom from your life of overwhelm.

PART I

THE COMMITMENT

CHAPTER 1

UNDERSTANDING OUR OVERWHELM

Although I do not know you, I am confident I know a lot about you. Chances are high that at some point throughout the week (or perhaps even throughout the day) you find yourself longing for a less stressful, simpler way of life. Your agenda is likely cluttered with meetings and events that drain your precious time and energy. And you likely have so many competing personal and professional priorities it is impossible to know what you should do first. Your responsibilities and obligations are never-ending, and rarely is anything on your to-do list for the benefit or betterment of yourself, which is why, even when you do complete a task or fulfill a commitment, *you* do not feel fulfilled.

When it comes to your village, your tribe by blood or friends chosen with love, you are connected to a lot of people. But far too often you find yourself wondering who among them truly appreciates you. Despite your continued allegiance, you cannot help but question if the real reason, if the *only* reason, you have so many connections is because of how much you do for others. Every time someone calls, you drop everything to be of service. But rarely, if ever, do you receive the same care in return.

When it comes to your work, you do not have to question whether your employers and colleagues have your best interests at heart. Deep down, you know the truth. You try not to get too upset because, after all, it is *just* a job. But for some reason, you have taken ownership of it. Somehow, you have come to believe it is *your* job, which is why you give so much of yourself, why you are so deeply committed even though you know the feeling isn't mutual. There is no comparison between how much you've given and how little you've received in exchange for your sacrifices.

In fact, much of what you do, no matter how altruistic, no longer gives you a sense of satisfaction. The hustle and bustle, the daily grind that used to excite you, has slowly crushed your soul. All the going and giving, all the ripping and running for others, has done nothing but drain your time, energy, and resources. You know that you should not be keeping score, that doing a mental tally of what you have done for others and what they haven't done for you only fuels your anger. But seriously, where is the reciprocity? Hell, you'd be grateful for a simple thank you!

At night you lie awake, exhausted and disappointed, because yet another day has passed where you have done the least to nothing at all for yourself. Yet again, instead of tending to your goals and dreams, you have catered to the needs of family members and friends. Yet again, you have spent your most productive hours helping others advance their missions and grow their businesses. Yet again, there is that bitter taste in your mouth, that chip on your shoulder, that resentment rising from the pit of your belly.

There are too many things you have to do and not enough time to do what you want to do. There are too many people who need you and not enough people who you can rely on in times of need. Being an adult feels like a trap, and you long to break free—from having too many things, too many priorities, too many obligations, too many personal relationships that feel transactional, and too many professional responsibilities where the work just ain't worth what you get in return.

You know you have too much on your plate, that you are doing the most, that you need to do less. You just do not know what to actually *do* about it!

So, you continue to do what you have always done: lie awake in the dark and stare at the ceiling, silently lamenting the injustice of it all until you fall asleep. Well, as you *try* to fall asleep. Because honestly, you have no way of knowing whether you drift off each night . . . or pass out from sheer exhaustion.

You might be wondering how I know you so well.

Surprise, surprise. I used to *be* you.

And the life of overwhelm that you are living used to be mine.

OUR LIVES OF THE MOST

Much like you, I once believed all the hype, that there were rewards to be had in hustling, and that having and doing all the things was the only road that led to happiness and success. Once upon a time, I too believed the fairy tale that there was real value in being seen as someone who could get shit done. Which is how I became a people pleaser, and a "get shit done with a smile" people pleaser at that.

Because I used to be so nice, so sweet, so kind, so caring, so nurturing, so humble, and so "just happy to be here." So inclined to just count my blessings that someone let me in the room so I could prove that I deserved to have a seat at the table. So willing to put others' needs before my own, personally and professionally. The people who have no problem asking others to do something for them *loved* to see me coming.

Now, when I reflect on these past seasons of my life at the height of overwhelm, here is what I find to be so unbelievable: no one *made* me move through the world this way. I was always "doing the most" because I *believed* I was supposed to. Largely because of what I'd been told or shown, directly or indirectly, by the caregivers and communities who raised me. So, despite my exhaustion, despite the shrinking and silent suffering, I never challenged what I'd been taught. I just continued to do what I'd always done: work twice as hard in the hope of being seen as half as good.

A LOVE NOTE TO BLACK WOMEN

Twice as Hard, Half as Good

Black women who are of a certain age live by certain rules that were lovingly passed down to us from generations before. Many baby boomers (born between 1946 and 1964), Generation Xers (born between 1965 and 1980), and perhaps even a few millennials (born between 1981 and 1996) were subjected to the same limiting belief: "You have to work twice as hard to be seen as half as good."

This guidance and similar Black proverbs were woven into our psyche at a young age, and we took them as gospel, believing that following suit would yield the promise of being seen and valued for our efforts. Which is why the belief that Black women need to work twice as hard to be seen as half as good continues to cause us so much harm. We work longer hours. We take on more tasks and responsibilities. We wear ourselves out in the hopes of being acknowledged and appreciated. All the while, we are setting unrealistic and unsustainable expectations for ourselves and other Black women in the workplace.

In *Our Separate Ways*, authors Ella L. J. Edmondson Bell and Stella M. Nkomo offer a deeply resonant truth that so many Black women know but rarely see reflected in mainstream discourse: The path to professional success is not only longer but also steeper for us.[1] We are often required to overperform, outwork, and outshine our peers just to be perceived as competent.[2] Bell and Nkomo highlight the origins and lived experiences of our complex relationship with doing the most: For many Black women, excellence isn't optional—it is expected, merely to gain entry into environments that were never built with us in mind. We tend to take great pride that, despite the odds being stacked against us, we continue to rise. But the real question we must ask ourselves is, At what cost?

Intuitively, we know that there is no amount of extra labor that can influence how employers determine our worth. And experience has taught us that nothing can change the hearts and minds of anyone determined to see us as inferior. Instead, working twice as hard in the hope of being seen as half as good and recognized for our greatness does nothing more than threaten our health and sanity. It is a limiting belief that is often at the root of neglecting ourselves—physically, mentally, emotionally, socially, and spiritually.

We must remember that much of our ancestral wisdom comes from a time when our people lived by adages that were rooted in navigating and surviving a racially stratified society, particularly under Jim Crow

and segregation. "You have to work twice as hard to be seen as half as good" is intergenerational wisdom that was intended to teach us to anticipate racial bias in public life—it was never intended to (nor do we have to) let it *dictate* our life and livelihoods.

Consider whether you may be harboring limiting beliefs that are a form of cultural survival strategy . . . and liberate yourself by letting those false narratives go.

Throughout college and early in my career, all the constant "doing the most" felt empowering, especially because I *did* seem to be reaping rewards for all my hard work. I got the best internships, the best jobs, the best titles, the best promotions, the best bonuses. And the best people-pleasing compliments:

I was driven.
I was motivated.
I was ambitious.
I was determined.
I was focused.
I was goal oriented.

I was all the toxic positivity that fuels capitalism and encourages grind culture.

And oh, how I thrived!

Well, at least publicly. Privately, the more I continued to advance in my career, the more I began to loathe having so little time and energy for myself. By the time I was in my mid- to late thirties, I hated the person I'd become—someone who just could not seem to say no to others, so I'd stopped saying yes to myself.

Perhaps, like me, you grew up unaware of the limiting beliefs that would one day govern your life. You may have been told to get a degree or a good job. Pursue a career, preferably with a coveted title. Earn a decent wage or six-figure salary. Commit to the perfect partner and have (or adopt) exceptional children (bonus points for also having an adorable pet!). Purchase an ideal property and fill all the rooms with all the things. Host gatherings to entertain family and friends. Take vacations every now and then (bonus points for posting the beautiful pictures on social media!). Retire and rest when your age is considered golden and your hair has turned gray.

Most of us believed (and may *still* believe) that some variation of this formula results in a happily ever after. Which is how our limiting beliefs become decrees that we live by—they are how we justify doing and having the most because we believe *this* is what it takes to have a fulfilling life. Unfortunately, it is often only *after* we've done all the "right" things that we find ourselves unable to shake the suspicion that we've done something wrong.

We have all the things, but nothing truly brings us joy.

We have mastered the art of prioritizing everything and everyone but ourselves.

We have enviable social calendars, but the events that pack our weeknights and weekends feel more obligatory than celebratory.

We have community, but our connections feel more transactional than genuine.

We make countless personal and professional sacrifices, hoping the stress will ultimately result in success. Instead, we find ourselves constantly overwhelmed by what it takes to sustain a dream we aren't even certain is ours. Instead, we learn there is a big difference between having a life that is full and being fulfilled by life.

overwhelm[3]

noun. the state in which there is too much on your plate, so much that it leads to anxiety, unhealthy stress, and burnout

Although we know that our lives of doing the most are the reason for our overwhelm, we rarely consider choosing less. That is largely because we tell ourselves this is what it takes to achieve our goals. And that is only part of the problem. Because overwhelm is not only representative of our exhaustion it is also the physical manifestation of being misaligned with our values and desires.

Overwhelm is not just about doing too much; it is about doing and having too much of what does not align with who we are, what we want, and what we deserve.

Of course, it is impossible to go through life without experiencing *any* overwhelm. Even if we are not overwhelmed by our day-to-day responsibilities, the unexpected can and does arise at the most inopportune times. So, everyone is bound to be extremely stressed at some point by something or someone. But there is a difference between feeling occasionally overwhelmed and feeling *constantly* overwhelmed.

"Overwhelm, like burnout, stress, and exhaustion, are all normal parts of life. An indicator of when these events are something more is when we cannot assign the feeling to a present and temporary circumstance, situation, or season. When navigating overwhelm is routine, then it is more than the normal occurrence. Instead, it is a state of being. And that is cause for concern."—Tieko Nejon Wilson, certified emotional intelligence practitioner

When we understand our overwhelm, we understand that it can teach us, often through discomfort, the difference between having a life full of things to do and be responsible for and being fulfilled by the choices we make in life. We understand that such lessons are not meant to cause disruption, but rather they are an invitation to pause and reassess our lives and livelihoods so that we can come into alignment. We understand that the life we are seeking freedom from can be a compass toward the life we are seeking freedom for.

Except, we *don't* understand our overwhelm.

Despite our discontent, despite feeling worn-out from sunup to sundown, if we do not understand our overwhelm it will never be cause for concern. At least, not enough for us to do something differently, not enough for us to change. Instead, living in a constant state of overwhelm can become our baseline. And whenever this happens, the question we must ask ourselves is why.

Achieving personal liberation requires us to confront ourselves—who we pretend to be versus who we desire to be. Because finding freedom from a life of overwhelm requires us to know not just who we are but, more importantly, *why* we are.

Why *do* we do what we do?

Why *do* we say what we say?

Why *do* we think what we think?

Why *do* we believe what we believe?

Asking ourselves why is the question that leads to understanding the reasons our lives are so overwhelming.

Why we do the most instead of doing less.

Why we say yes when we really want to say no.

Why we think and care so much about what others think about us.

Why we feel trapped in the lives we are seeking freedom from instead of pursuing the lives we are seeking freedom for.

Why is more than a general ask—it is a radical question of self-inquiry. It is an invitation to pause, stop living our lives on autopilot, and become conscious participants. There is power in knowing why we are doing something, agreeing to something, or tolerating something, especially those things that do not align with who we are or desire to be. Because somewhere, embedded deep within each why, is a limiting belief that is governing our decision to make choices to our own detriment.

> Limiting beliefs are restrictive convictions about oneself that can hinder personal growth and achievement. These beliefs often develop through a combination of early life experiences, cultural and societal influences, and personal interpretations of events. Repeated exposure to negative feedback or criticism, especially during formative years, can lead individuals to internalize these limiting beliefs, affecting their self-perception and behavior over time.[4]

Once we understand how our limiting beliefs quietly shape our choices, we begin to understand just how much power they hold over our lives (and overwhelm!). Our internal narratives—often inherited, unchallenged, or the result of past experiences—can keep us stuck in cycles of abandoning ourselves. The good news? What we have learned to believe over time can be unlearned. And the moment we commit to questioning these hidden truths is the moment we begin to reclaim our personal freedom.

THE POWER OF OUR LIMITING BELIEFS

No one is born with limiting beliefs about themselves. Nor do we ever imagine ourselves to engage in limiting behaviors like people-pleasing and self-sacrificing. We may not even realize that our actions are a reflection of us desperately seeking others' approval. We *become* this way based on our exposure to psychological, social, and environmental factors, and usually through no fault of our own. Our caregivers, our communities, and even the popular social constructs of our childhood were instrumental in determining how we view ourselves in relation to others and the spaces we inhabit.

With the exception of abusive and controlling dynamics, it is important to note that people often have no idea that their words or actions are causing someone else to form a limiting belief. On the contrary, we may think we are providing useful feedback or giving constructive criticism. We tend to think we are being helpful, providing words of wisdom, or that our honest critique will be a source of encouragement to do better or try harder the next time. But what we have really done is plant a narrative that has the power to become an insecurity or lead to self-doubt in the same way we came to harbor our own limiting beliefs: A messenger, knowingly or unknowingly, gave us the wrong message.

When a Messenger Gives Us the Wrong Message

The messenger is the source of any narrative that influences or impacts our confidence and self-worth. The messenger can be a person, members of a community or collective, or even an institution. It is *anyone* or *anything* we hold in high regard or respect enough to want their love, validation, or approval. Of course, we encounter many messengers in our lifetime. And their words and actions don't always leave a lasting impression. It is when messengers' narratives have the power to sway what we believe about ourselves that they become problematic—the wrong message. Whenever a messenger gives us the wrong message and it becomes deeply ingrained, we form limiting beliefs that govern how we move through the world.

During our formative years, we are more likely to be subjected to limiting beliefs because we are constantly being "taught" something by our caregivers and communities. Throughout childhood and young adulthood, we are like sponges as we soak up expectations and unspoken rules from the people and environments around us. Because we are still developing our sense of identity and are (mostly) deferential to authority figures, we are especially vulnerable to internalizing what we are told and shown as fact. We have no clue we are soaking up the wrong messages that will ultimately shape how we see ourselves and what we believe we deserve, and determine how much we are willing to sacrifice to belong.

Even though many of our limiting beliefs form in our youth, it is important to note that we can develop limiting beliefs at any point in our lifetime. Remember, all it takes is a messenger—someone or some form of authority we respect or hold dear—to give us the wrong message that impacts our confidence. Believe it or not, even we ourselves can even be the messenger! This is why it so important to be mindful of what we tell ourselves and how we frame our personal experiences, especially those that leave a lasting impression. Constantly berating instead of forgiving ourselves is yet another way we form limiting beliefs.

Although you may be tempted to home in on the messengers who gave you the wrong messages, please know there is less power in being able to name who told us what, where, when, and why. We cannot undo what happened, we can only do the work to unlearn and move forward. The *real* power is in being able to identify our limiting beliefs:

If I slow down, I'll fall behind.
If I don't do it, no one else will.
If I don't go, I'll disappoint them.
If I say no, they'll say I'm selfish.
If I'm not busy, I'm not doing enough.

The sooner we identify our limiting beliefs, the sooner we begin to see clearly how they keep us tethered to going and doing and producing and giving of ourselves beyond our capacity. And we begin the necessary work of letting go of the notion that this is the only way we will be seen, valued, or loved. Because every time we replace the wrong messages we received with the right ones, we take back our power and start to find freedom from our lives of overwhelm.

GENERATIONAL LIMITING BELIEFS

It should come as no surprise that identifying our limiting beliefs will take us down memory lane. We may immediately pinpoint some of the wrong messages we received, while others require a little more introspection. A great place to start is by reflecting on your childhood more generally—considering statements and expectations that were shaped by the social constructs of your time—before turning your attention to more specific or personal experiences. This is a gentle way to begin the inner work of self-assessment, which can be difficult at times. You can also discuss generational limiting beliefs with siblings or friends, which may elevate some of the stigma or shame that often arises.

Please know that nothing is wrong with you for having limiting beliefs, nor did you do anything wrong by allowing them to dictate your life thus far. You were simply unaware or, if you were somewhat aware of the wrong messages you received, you may not have fully understood their power. An exploration of generational limiting beliefs will provide additional insight and, hopefully, allow you to show yourself some compassion. You will understand how it is nearly impossible to *not* have at least one internalized narrative that can hinder your personal growth. Because, without question, every generation receives its fair share of wrong messages. Consider whether any of the following generational limiting beliefs may have influenced your life of overwhelm.

Baby Boomers (1946–1964): Living the American Dream

This generation focused on achieving the "American Dream." The dominant limiting belief? People had to follow the same linear path to success—college, marriage, homeownership, and retirement. Because television shows like *Leave It to Beaver* and popular magazines like *Good Housekeeping* depicted ideal suburban lifestyles, baby boomers' limiting beliefs centered on stability:

> *If I don't own a home and have a solid career and a nuclear family, I have failed in life.*

Baby boomers who internalized these limiting beliefs found it difficult to deviate from living the American Dream, no matter how personally unfulfilling or overwhelming. As a result, their children were susceptible to internalizing limiting beliefs around stability—directly or indirectly—and as adults struggled to depart from their parents' definition of success:

> *I hate this job, but I can't leave. It's stable, solid. I'd be a fool to walk away to pursue entrepreneurship.*
>
> *I cannot believe I am* still *renting an apartment. I should really own a house by now.*
>
> *Ugh! When am I going to find my partner? I need to get married and have babies before I'm too old!*

For baby boomers, any success that does not reflect their understanding of stability—a good job, a good salary, a good car, a good partner, and a good plan for retirement—seems fleeting. (But in all fairness, we *should* cut baby boomers a little slack here. After all, their limiting beliefs were shaped by personal stories and tragedies around the instability of the Great Depression.)

Generation X (1965–1980): Me, Myself, and I

As a seventies baby, I can speak with authority about my generation's limiting beliefs. We were free-range children who played and stayed outside until the streetlights came on. We did our chores to earn our keep—to have a roof over our heads, clothes on our backs, and shoes on our feet—*not* to receive an allowance. We wore house keys on strings around our necks, took food out of the freezer to thaw when we got home from school, and, if need be, cooked dinner for ourselves and our younger siblings before our caregivers' workday ended.

As the last generation to experience the joys of Saturday morning cartoons and life before the internet, we Gen Xers love to romanticize our childhood. But the truth is, many of us "latchkey kids" had to learn to be self-sufficient as a form of survival way too young. Popular culture reinforced this as the norm, especially after-school television programming. As a result,

Gen Xers entered adulthood with limiting beliefs centered on hyper-independence:

I have to do everything on my own.

We struggle to ask for support and likewise struggle to receive it when it's offered, which is why Gen Xers often find themselves overwhelmed by trying to do it all:

I can't ask for help. That will make me look weak.

I don't need anybody. Besides, you can't trust people anyway.

I'll just do whatever I need to do to get the job done. That's what I've always done.

Surprisingly (or perhaps, not surprisingly), unlike baby boomers, who drilled limiting beliefs about the American Dream into their children, many Gen Xers took a different approach. In an attempt to heal their own childhood trauma, they were determined their children would never have to be hyper-independent. Instead, they were intentional about making sure their children felt heavily nurtured. This, I would be remiss not to mention, has caused a common concern among Gen X parents: whether we *over* course-corrected by making life *too easy* for our children.

Millennials (1981–1996): Hustle, and Hustle Hard

Even though I am a Gen Xer, since I was a mere five years old in 1981, I was certainly privy to my fair share of millennials' limiting beliefs. This is the generation that defined grind culture, that glorified personal sacrifice as a symbol of success. Millennials' limiting beliefs center on wearing burnout like a badge of honor.

I have to be productive to prove my worth.

Millennials are known for pushing through despite feeling overwhelmed. From television programming to social media platforms, millennials were constantly bombarded with messaging that rest was for the weak and lazy, and productivity was the key to getting ahead:

Sleep? You can sleep when you're dead!

Only in recent years have millennials come to understand rest as a requirement and not a reward. As parents, they have also taken great care to ensure their children benefit from the fruits of their labor. Likewise, many millennial parents share the same concerns as Gen Xers: whether they caused more harm than good by allowing their children to experience the lifestyle of leisure they secretly longed for in their youth.

Generation Z (1997–2012): Look at Me. Follow Me.

Although the newest generation has many modern conveniences, growing up in a hyper-digital world is not without its own fair share of concerns. This is the first generation to have their self-worth and success defined by a strong online presence or large social media following (despite it being widely known that much of this is beyond their control). Gen Zers often express having anxiety about being irrelevant online . . . or becoming relevant for all the wrong reasons.[5]

The most prevalent limiting belief internalized by Gen Zers:

If I am not seen, I do not matter.

This is my daughter's generation, and we had many visibility-as-validation conversations during her teenage years. I also remember how overwhelming it was to maintain an online presence as the Afrominimalist. So much so that I ultimately changed my handle to reclaim my time and identity! Establishing and maintaining an online presence as a form of social currency isn't easy, and this is especially true for Gen Zers, who are extremely self-conscious and heavily dependent on peer validation.[6] This is why they often find it incredibly difficult to follow the guidance of their parents and caregivers to simply ignore others' opinions.[7]

Now you understand why even though I do not know you, I know a lot about you. I do not need to know the messengers you encountered, or the details about the wrong messages you received to know that you have limiting beliefs that are the source of your overwhelm.

They are the reason you say yes when you really want to say no.

They are the reason you think and care so much about others' opinions of you.

They are the reason you do and have the most instead of embracing a life with less.

I do not need to know you because I know myself—who I used to be, the life I used to live, and why.

What the journey to personal liberation taught me is that at the heart of every limiting belief is the same internalized lie: *I am not worthy unless. . . .* And I know that until we commit to honoring ourselves by letting go of this false narrative, we will continue to live in a constant state of overwhelm. Unfortunately, I also know firsthand the toll such a life takes on our well-being—physically, mentally, emotionally, socially, and spiritually.

WE ARE UNWELL

For years, saying "I am so overwhelmed" was my go-to response whenever someone asked how I was doing. This statement had replaced its predecessors, “I am so stressed” and “I am so tired,” which had long since lost their meaning. Overwhelm had a certain *je ne sais quoi* to it. Something that made it sound more respectable than mere stress. Every limiting belief I had about my value being tied to people-pleasing and productivity made *saying* I was overwhelmed sound important and even a little sexy . . . until an annual checkup with my primary care physician forced me to acknowledge the ugly truth.

What I thought would be a routine annual checkup brought to light a rather scary diagnosis: high blood pressure. High stage 2 hypertension, to be exact. I was forty-seven years old, barely middle age! Yet I was on the borderline of being in a hypertensive crisis that required immediate medical attention. What was most terrifying? I had absolutely no idea anything was wrong.

I still remember how I felt that morning as I sat in disbelief while the nurse went to find the cardiac specialist. (I didn't even know my doctor's office had a cardiac specialist!) Meanwhile, my doctor began asking me a series of questions in a very serious tone as she took another blood pressure reading:

“So, you drove yourself to this appointment?”

“Yes.”

“And you felt fine the entire drive? No issues, nothing alarming or out of the ordinary?”

“Nope, nothing.”

As someone who once considered my car my second office, as usual, I'd spent the entire drive on a conference call. I'd offered sound advice, gave recommendations. It had been business as usual.

“And right now, you feel fine?”

“Yes.”

“You don't feel weak? Or like anything is off?”

“Nope.”

“Do you feel like you can drive yourself home?”

“Yes. I feel fine!”

Honestly, I also recall feeling slightly annoyed because I wanted to check my email, and there was no way I could dig into my handbag while wearing a blood pressure cuff, which, in hindsight, is much more problematic than it seemed at the time.

The cardiac specialist arrived and, perhaps sensing my irritation, let me know why the team was being as thorough as possible with their questioning and multiple pressure readings: "We are trying to determine whether we should prescribe medication and send you home . . . or send you directly to the ER."

Umm, excuse me? The emergency room?

There was no way this was happening, because I felt *fine*!

Oh, I should also note that I looked fine too. I'd always been model-thin and had been taught to dress my best for medical appointments, so I certainly did not *look* like a woman on the verge of having a stroke or heart attack. However, as I listened and learned about the symptoms of hypertension, I realized I *had* experienced some of the telltale signs over the past several months. But I'd self-diagnosed my occasional dizziness and blurred vision as exhaustion, hunger, or the common catchall for a woman in her late forties: perimenopause.

After handing me a one-pager that listed the standard lifestyle recommendations to reduce salt intake, limit alcohol consumption, and exercise more often, the cardiac specialist said, "Given your medical history, it seems your high blood pressure is most likely stress-related. What are the stressors in your life? Work? Financial? Family issues?" She lowered her voice, leaned in, and whispered, "Is it a relationship? Your partner?"

A relationship? A partner? Who had the time?!

Every parent has their pandemic struggle stories, and I was in the lot of those trying to navigate my daughter's senior year of high school, first year of college, and *my* first year as an empty nester during that unprecedented time. It had been hell. For both of us. But we'd survived. The world—*our worlds*—had returned to a state of somewhat normalcy. I'd also started to embrace *my* new normal—being solely responsible for myself.

After spending nearly two decades mothering and schlepping all over Washington, DC, for my daughter's violin practices and performances, my time was all mine again! Well, sort of.

"It's my job." I confessed to the cardiac specialist, surprised myself that there was only one stressor in my life. "Everything else is manageable, ideal really."

"Your *job*?" my primary doctor interrupted, unable to hide her surprise. "I thought you were writing full-time now that your daughter's away at college. What happened?"

Yes, I had transitioned to being a full-time writer. But since my last annual checkup, I'd also taken on a full-time job with an organization that needed a fixer. Thanks to my limiting beliefs, trying to "fix" anything (and anyone) that was broken had always been a people-pleasing sweet spot of mine.

The new job required my full devotion. I worked early mornings, late nights, and weekends, just like I had during my years in Big Law. The overwhelm felt familiar, and I felt great every time I received praise for solving a problem. Before I knew it, I wasn't just fixing the organization's infrastructure; I was building it. And the toll it had taken was clearly reflected in my blood pressure readings.

"Your . . . *job*." The cardiac specialist frowned. "Well, I really want you to think about that."

And trust me, I did think about it. Nonstop.

I thought about the toll of overwhelm on my way to pick up my blood pressure medication. I'd have to take it every day, perhaps for the rest of my life, which instantly made me feel closer to old age than middle age.

I thought about the toll of overwhelm on my way home as I called my closest friends with the sad news about my new medical condition. They were equally shocked, because I appeared so healthy. And since my doctor recommended that I cut back on drinking, we couldn't make a beeline to happy hour to cheer me up.

I thought about the toll of overwhelm as I sat on my sofa and cried, wondering not if, but when, I might have had a stroke or something worse had I not *finally* made time for my annual checkup.

I thought about the toll of overwhelm as I resigned from my job. Because there was no role, no mission or work, no matter how impactful, that was worth compromising my health.

Suddenly, I had an ample amount of something I'd always found some way to fill: time.

Time to take leisurely walks. Time to take long naps. Time to have slow afternoons with my aging mother and extended college visits with my daughter, instead of always being in a rush. Time to catch up with friends, to have lengthy conversations and meetups instead of sending "Sorry, I'm so busy!" texts. Time to think about how I'd felt fine the day I learned I had high blood pressure, and how I'd looked "Black don't crack" fine too. And how scary it was that I'd had no idea anything was wrong.

Because overwhelm had become my baseline.

A LOVE NOTE TO BLACK WOMEN

Black ~~Don't~~ Does Crack . . .

From Maya Angelou celebrating us as phenomenal women to Beyoncé singing about the joy of being a brown-skinned girl, there are many poems and songs that honor the undeniable beauty of Black women. Despite the hardships that accompany our diverse hues, Black women love being Black women. And we love reminding ourselves and others about the benefits of our melanated skin by saying, "Black don't crack." And while this is true for most Black women as they age, what is happening on a cellular level is less impressive and far more concerning.

Because we *are* cracking . . . internally.

Yes, all humans suffer from the same health conditions associated with capitalism, including but not limited to chronic stress and fatigue, depression and anxiety, diabetes, and high blood pressure[8] (just to name a few!). But Black Americans are also victims to intersectional systems of oppression that can accelerate underlying medical issues. Within academia, this well-established public health concern is known as "weathering," a term coined by Dr. Arline T. Geronimus to explain the toll systemic racism and oppression takes on the body.

Black bodies age faster. Black bodies deteriorate more rapidly. Black bodies have higher rates of chronic illnesses and diseases. Black bodies have higher rates of premature death. And these statistics are irrespective of our social status and socioeconomic achievements. As Dr. Geronimus so plainly and painfully stated in her findings, "Health is not an immutable consequence of one's genetic code, nor a reflection of one's character. Living life according to the dominant social norms of personal responsibility and virtue is not universally health promoting. On the contrary: if you're Black, working hard and playing by the rules can be part of what kills you."[9]

Weathering is a hidden toll, one that others cannot see but that Black Americans are constantly carrying, and it heavily impacts the well-being of Black women. Rarely does anyone know how much doing the most is wearing on us. Rarely do we even express to one another how the toll of Black women *really* feels. And not because we don't want to; rather because being forthcoming about our challenges with wellness is a new space we are navigating. Surely there are a few exceptions but the majority of the women who raised us did not have the luxury of prioritizing their well-being. So we never saw them take steps to reduce their overwhelm. Instead, we often saw the Black women in our lives push through their pain to provide for themselves and their families. We saw them do what they had to do to survive . . . and admired their ability to not "look like" what they'd been through.

Black women have been conditioned to keep doing more, to keep working hard and playing by the rules. To keep "pushing through" as if our survival still depends on it, and to make sure we look flawless while doing it. But we must learn to be intentional about caring for our *whole* well-being—not just looking good but also *feeling* good. Otherwise we risk our Black "cracking" on the inside as we continue weathering our minds, bodies, and souls.

Consider whether you may be harboring limiting beliefs that cause you to care more about your outward appearance than your overall health, and liberate yourself by letting those false narratives go.

According to recent studies, the average age of Black women who have a stroke is around fifty-seven years old, which is significantly younger than the average age for white women (around seventy-five).[10] As daunting as that disparity is, I can honestly say it did not hit as hard as the health conversations I had with family members and friends. It seemed everyone had a story—personal or that of a former classmate or colleague—of experiencing life-altering (or life-ending) medical emergencies resulting from extreme stress. Hearing others' stories made me only more thankful that my story didn't have a different ending. And I became ever more intentional about prioritizing myself.

After receiving a referral from my dear friend and wellness practitioner Yasmine Cheyenne, I scheduled an appointment with Dr. Gelane Gemechisa, an integrative health doctor in the Washington, DC, area, affectionately known as Dr. G. I was hopeful she could help me stabilize my blood pressure (and manage the depression the diagnosis had caused) without the aid of prescription drugs.

All I could do was hope that integrative health care would live up to its hype. Unlike alternative medicine, which is often used in lieu of conventional health care, integrative health doctors work *with* primary care physicians to provide a comprehensive, holistic approach to their patients' health care and well-being. Within the first ten minutes of meeting Dr. G, I became a believer.

Rather than immediately having to undress and slip into an annoyingly thin paper gown, I remained fully clothed. Instead of spending the majority of my appointment on a hard examination table, I sat in a comfy chair opposite Dr. G's desk as she spent the first forty minutes of our time together asking about my life—not just my medical history. And not just asking but also, and more importantly, listening closely to my answers.

From my childhood to young adulthood to motherhood to being an unemployed empty nester racked with shame about having high blood pressure from work-induced stress, we talked about *everything*. Still, nothing could have prepared me for her diagnosis.

"Christine, you are unwell," Dr. G said.

All I could do was cry.

unwell[11]

noun. a state of being in which a person feels physically or mentally ill, unhealthy, or generally not in good health

When I tell you that diagnosis hit me hard? My focus immediately shifted away from getting off high blood pressure medication and antidepressants. The only thing I wanted to do was be well!

"Most people are unwell," Dr. G explained as she handed me a box of tissues. "They just aren't aware of it. The beautiful thing is that you can and *will* get better. Because our bodies are always, *always* trying to be well. We just have to learn to listen."

Then Dr. G asked, "Christine, have you ever heard of the Five Foundations of Wellness?"

It was the question that changed both my life and the course of this book.

The Five Foundations of Wellness is a diagnostic paradigm widely used in traditional, alternative, and integrative medicine to assess a patient's health. It takes into consideration the state of our physical, emotional, mental, social, and spiritual health to determine our overall well-being.

Our *physical health* is assessed by the state of our body, including but not limited to daily movement and exercise, and whether we are getting proper nutrition and adequate rest. Our *emotional health* is determined by how well we understand, manage, and express our feelings. Our *mental or intellectual health* takes into consideration our ability to learn, grow, and foster creativity as well as our ability to maintain and strengthen our problem-solving skills. Our *social health* is evaluated by the strength of our romantic and interpersonal relationships, and whether we feel supported by the communities in which we live and serve. Last, our *spiritual health* is assessed not only by our religion or faith-based practices but also by whether we are doing meaningful work and feel we are living a meaningful life.[12]

If any one of these foundations of health is compromised, a patient is deemed unwell. Because to be well, we need all aspects of our well-being—physical, emotional, mental, social, and spiritual—to be at optimal levels.

While it may sound dramatic, I am convinced that my appointment with Dr. G not only forever changed my life but also saved it. As my wellness journey began, I found myself referencing the Five Foundations paradigm regularly. So much so that I began to envision each foundation of wellness as its own Personal Well. I was determined to make myself and my health a priority . . . one foundation at a time.

Checking on my Personal Wells became a simple way for me to check in with myself and my well-being.

I took note of everything—what I did, what I ate, who I talked to and hung out with, how I felt—to determine who and what drained my Personal Wells. And even more importantly, who and what filled them (and me) to optimal levels. For the first time in my life, I had a way to listen to what my body was trying to tell and show me. And whenever I found myself struggling to listen, I asked myself why. Without fail, there was always some limiting belief trying to convince me that I had to prioritize others' needs over my own.

I began to understand the power of my limiting beliefs and how they impacted not just my to-do list but also how I felt from day to day. Listening to some of the stories I told myself about why I should or shouldn't and could or couldn't do something became lessons in and of themselves. Because how could I not have enough time to:

- Eat, sleep, or go for a walk and fill my Physical Well?
- Take a break to process my feelings and fill my Emotional Well?

- Read or listen to an audiobook and fill my Mental Well?
- Spend time with loved ones and fill my Social Well?
- Daydream or write stories and fill my Spiritual Well?
- How could I not have enough time to care for my well-being but enough time to do all the things for others?

I became more adept at recognizing, challenging, and letting go of my limiting beliefs. But of course, there were many moments where I had to learn these lessons the hard way. Because whenever I did give in to seeking approval or not wanting to disappoint others, I found myself overwhelmed and exhausted from draining my Personal Wells.

Overwhelm, it seems, is our body's way of telling us that it is time to stop doing the most, that we need to choose less so we have the time to commit to the daily work of honoring ourselves. It is our body's way of letting us know that we are unwell. And because our bodies are always, *always* trying to help us be well, we are always receiving signs and having symptoms whenever some aspect of our physical, emotional, mental, social, or spiritual health needs our immediate attention. It seems there are only a few things powerful enough to override our innate desire to care for ourselves: the limiting beliefs we have about ourselves.

So again, even though I do not know you, I know a lot about you. And I know that you *can* and *will* find freedom from your life of overwhelm. Because you, my friend, are both the source and solution to your liberation.

CHAPTER 2

THE LIFE YOU'RE SEEKING FREEDOM FROM

Understanding overwhelm as more than just a stress response allowed me to reflect on life through a new lens. I could clearly see how my limiting beliefs caused me to do the most throughout my career as well as how they'd shaped my personal and professional relationships. I could no longer ignore how often I'd allowed my Personal Wells to become depleted, nor the pain of how I'd spent years neglecting myself by prioritizing and pleasing others.

Even though I did not know it, I'd been seeking freedom from my overwhelming life for a long time. And there was one day I thought about more than any other.

Ah, that fateful morning five years into my career when I woke up feeling more overwhelmed than when I'd gone to bed just a few hours before. When I'd picked up my cellphone, hoping to distract myself with a game of Brick Breaker,* only to be bombarded by dozens of email notifications awaiting my response. I looked around the house, panicked by everything I needed to do to be a good parent before I went to work to be a good employee

---

* I'm a Gen Xer, okay? And despite the overwhelm it caused me, the Blackberry remains one of the best work phones ever invented.

while also, somehow, being a good wife, a good friend, and a good daughter to my aging mother, who I'd recently relocated to the area.

That morning, I did what any logical overwhelmed person might do: I went to Google and typed in the three words I hoped would change my life: "how to disappear."

Oh, c'mon! Do not tell me that you have not at least *thought* about pulling a disappearing act at some point in your overwhelming life.

Envisioning yourself smiling as you pack up your favorite things and essentials into a simple backpack. Slipping into your favorite pair of comfy sweats. Lacing up those still-like-new hiking boots that you've only worn once because you never have time to take a hike. Walking off into the sunset, never to be seen or heard from again.

Well, at least that is what *I* imagined the morning I longed to escape everything I had to do and everyone who needed me to do something for them.

As soon as I tapped "search," hundreds of blog posts from survivalists populated the screen. Smiling and excited, I reached for the pen and to-do list on my nightstand and flipped to a blank page, ready to take notes. But alas, it did not take long for me to realize that my search had yielded some rather disappointing results.

Turns out, it is incredibly complicated to disappear.

Of course, there were legal consequences. Plus, the financial burden of needing to have plenty of cash on hand so that purchases could not be tracked. Then, there was the emotional toll of never being able to contact loved ones ever again. I had a beautiful community that I was blessed to call my chosen family, and article after article confirmed they'd never stop searching for me, which meant *I* would never be able to stop fluctuating my weight and donning cheap colorful wigs to disguise my appearance.

Let's just say, the more I read about what I would have to do if I wanted to disappear and never be found, the more heartbroken I became. Even if I was willing to take the risks and run away from my overwhelming life, I'd *still* have stuff to do.

Geez!

Turns out, I am not the only person to have considered taking such a drastic measure. Perhaps you may have even considered it yourself. If you have, just know you (and I) are not alone. Just as feeling overwhelmed by the pressures of life is not a new phenomenon, neither are the extremes that people consider in the hopes of escaping. And the lengths to which some people go extend far beyond googling how to disappear.

> "In 2023, more than 563,000 missing person reports were recorded by the National Crime Information Center, a database run by the FBI and comprised of criminal data, including missing persons cases involving minors and adults. For about half of those cases, optional criteria were used to help classify a person's disappearance as an abduction or voluntary, according to an NCIC report. Of those cases, approximately 95% were labeled as runaways."—Amanda Musa, CNN[1]

While we tend to hear more sensationalized stories about wealthy tycoons trying to evade mounting debt or drug lords on the lam, the reality is that everyday people also try to escape their overwhelming lives.

Every.

Single.

Day.

Which is what Esther Beadle tried to do on Friday, January 29, 2016.[2]

When Esther vanished from the popular suburban village of Cowley in Oxford, England, she could have easily been described as a well-rounded, well-established woman in her twenties. A respected assistant editor at the *Oxford Mail*, she was on the fast track to have a successful career in journalism. With her striking features and warm, welcoming smile, Esther and her boyfriend made for a stunning couple, and she was certain she'd found the person—*her* person—to share her life with. She also had a loving and supportive network . . . and they went into overdrive the day she failed to arrive for a planned meetup.

Believing she had been kidnapped or met some other unfortunate fate, Esther's family and friends went to local law enforcement to have her deemed a missing person. A frantic search ensued. Her pictures were posted throughout Cowley and were later featured on the news. For nearly three excruciating days, the search for Esther intensified. Until suddenly, she reappeared and surrendered herself to law enforcement.

Those two fateful decisions—first, to momentarily disappear and, later, to turn herself in to authorities—resulted in Esther losing nearly every interpersonal relationship she held dear, including her romantic partnership. As more news outlets highlighted Esther's not-really-a-missing-person case, the public commentary was so damning that she also lost her job. By the end of the ordeal, Esther felt she had no choice but to move away from the Cowley community she loved.

Esther gave an interview about her ordeal, and many people were surprised by her perspective of what had transpired: She was, in fact, *not* missing during that brief window of time when no one could find her—she'd just needed a break.

"In my eyes, people were missing from me," Esther shared. "I'd removed myself from everything, to try to push the world away."

While it may be tempting to judge Esther's choices and the unfortunate aftermath as "what she deserved," I find it rather commendable that Esther did what so many others who have gone missing have not done—return to face the consequences of her actions. Because the truth is, she merely followed through on a common impulse people have when overwhelmed by the pressures in their lives: a longing to be free.

> "It is not uncommon for adults with full lives to have passive thoughts about walking away from everything they know . . . [which speaks to] the great level of overwhelm people are feeling. They don't always know easy solutions to their problems, and so then they do find themselves wanting to run away and escape it all."—Dr. Lauren Cook, clinical psychologist[3]

Although most people are too afraid to follow through on voluntarily going missing, there are many other ways that we, knowingly or unknowingly, try to escape our feelings of being unable to cope. In "Avoidance Behavior: Examples, Impacts, and How to Overcome," mental health clinician Silvi Saxena defines avoidant behaviors as "any action people use to escape or distract themselves from difficult thoughts, feelings, and situations."[4] This may look like:

The emails we delay answering.
The envelopes we delay opening.
The places we refuse to go.
The people we refuse to see.
The aches and pains we ignore, hoping they will just go away.

Throughout our lives, we have all used avoidance as a momentary escape from the inevitable. Being avoidant is a common coping mechanism for good reason—it gives us the *illusion* of control until we feel ready to deal with the matter at hand. But if we are not careful, avoidance has a way of making matters worse.

That fateful morning I googled "how to disappear" was avoidance at its finest. Because what I really needed to do that morning was face the truth: Living in a constant state of overwhelm had made me unwell. So unwell that I'd searched online about doing something I now would consider unthinkable! Clearly, my Mental Well was drained, but so were other aspects of my well-being. But because overwhelm was my baseline, because my limiting beliefs were dictating how I should manage my life, I had no idea about any of it.

The truth is, I had no idea I was unwell because I did not know what it meant to *be* well.

OUR WELLS, OUR WELL-BEING

From reflecting on how I had considered pulling a disappearing act early in my career to revisiting how I felt the day of my shocking hypertension diagnosis and the months spent in recovery focusing on my Personal Wells, I could not help but wonder: Why *are* so many people unwell? And if our bodies are always, *always* trying to help us, why is it so hard to *be* well?

Prior to my appointment with an integrative health doctor, beyond drinking as much water as possible and attending yoga and spin classes, wellness was not something that I gave much thought to. I mean, I ate as well as I could, but also indulged in the best (and worst) of meals. I loved a good nap just as much as I loved a good late night out with friends. I went to therapy, and whether it be prescription meds or medicinals, I had no qualms about discussing or managing my mental health. I had a beautiful village, an eclectic group of friends who ranged from their early twenties to late seventies. Our daily conversations and interactions allowed me to express my range of emotions. Although I was minimalist with my wardrobe, I was a spiritual "woo woo" maximalist with more incense, candles, and crystals than any one woman should have. Best of all, I'd found what I believed to be my calling—being a storyteller—and my career was flourishing.

That is to say, I had all the resources and blessings to keep my Personal Wells at optimal levels . . . yet I was *still* overwhelmed and unwell. And I likely would have remained that way until I learned what it meant to *be* well.

It is hard to believe that for generations, wellness was intuitive. Rooted in community, wellness rituals and practices were once passed down through our familial, cultural, and spiritual belief systems. Wellness was not something we had to seek out—it was embedded in our daily life, woven into the rhythms of each season, and passed down generationally through the wisdom of our elders. People just lived in ways that naturally aligned with prioritizing wellness and overall well-being.

Our sleep cycles followed a circadian rhythm that aligned with sunrise and sunset. This was also true of our work schedules prior to the invention of the clock. Likewise, it was easy for our bodies to regularly be in motion. Without trains, planes, and automobiles, we walked, traveled by horseback or buggy, or rode bicycles. Before the emergence of grocery stores, we grew our own food, and what we didn't grow or use, we bought or bartered for with others. And most common ailments were healed with home remedies.

Simply put, wellness was not something we had to put much thought into—it was just a way of life.

However, over time, colonization, industrialization, and the rise of modern medicine began to displace (and more recently, *replace*) our ancestral ways of knowing. Wellness became medicalized, commodified, and increasingly individualized, which separated us from the holistic, communal foundations that once guided our care. And now here we are, so disconnected from ourselves and practices that can heal us that overwhelm can feel like a healthy, normal baseline.

Less Is Liberation is an invitation to remember and reimagine some of these timeless principles in ways that feel both rooted and relevant. Because wellness is *still* intuitive. Our bodies are still always, always trying to tell and show us when we are unwell. We just have to (re)learn how to listen. And choosing less is a simple way to start reclaiming our time and agency over our well-being.

Now that you have a better understanding of overwhelm as well as the power of limiting beliefs, let's explore the ways in which they collectively impact our health. When left unaddressed, overwhelm can trigger a prolonged stress response in the body, affecting everything from our sleep and digestion to our immune system and hormonal balance. And when we allow our limiting beliefs to dictate our capacity—beliefs that tell us we can't slow down, rest is lazy, or that we can't be selfish—we can easily find ourselves dealing with the repercussions of self-neglect. Over time, the impact of our internal narratives coupled with external pressures can manifest as anxiety, burnout, emotional exhaustion and, as I know all too well, physical illness.

HOW LIMITING BELIEFS IMPACT OUR WELL-BEING

The Need to Be Perfect

Limiting Belief: "If I don't do everything perfectly, I will fail."

Limiting Behavior: Spending excessive time and energy trying to meet unrealistic standards and expectations.

How It Impacts Our Well-Being: Keeps us constantly striving, afraid to rest, and never feeling like enough.

The Need for Approval

Limiting Belief: "I must keep everyone happy so they will love me."

Limiting Behavior: Saying yes when we want to say no; sacrificing our well-being to satisfy others.

How It Impacts Our Well-Being: Leaves us depleted, resentful, and without time for ourselves.

The Need to Be Productive

Limiting Belief: "My worth is tied to how much I accomplish."

Limiting Behavior: Filling every moment with tasks, feeling guilty when we rest.

How It Impacts Our Well-Being: Creates a relentless cycle of work, leaving no space for joy, creativity, or reflection.

The Fear of Change

Limiting Belief: "It's safer to stay where I am, even if I'm unhappy."

Limiting Behavior: Staying in misaligned jobs, relationships, or routines out of fear of the unknown.

How It Impacts Our Well-Being: Keeps us trapped in dissatisfaction, draining our energy and wasting our most precious finite resource: our time.

By understanding the connection between how we feel and what we believe about ourselves, we begin to see that being well isn't just about how we look and feel physically—it requires us to be mentally, emotionally, socially, and spiritually healthy too. If wellness is the practice of aligning our daily life with our core values and needs, being well is the work of honoring that alignment with intention, compassion, and consistency. And this is why using the Personal Wells framework as a self-assessment tool can help you find freedom from your life of overwhelm *and* freedom for a life that honors your well-being.

OUR PERSONAL WELLS

Imagine yourself as the beautiful vessel of life that you are. Your Personal Wells are what fill that vessel. They are the areas of your health that make you function at optimal capacity, but if they are not properly cared for, they can also leave you feeling drained and overwhelmed. It's your responsibility to tend to your Wells, to check on their levels regularly and lovingly supply them with what they need. Keep in mind that you may already be filling your Personal Wells daily—knowingly or unknowingly—based on your habits and routines.

The Physical Well

The Physical Well is representative of our body. It is perhaps the most important of our Personal Wells as it is indeed the main vessel that supports the other areas of our health. Ironically, it is the Well we tend to neglect the most, believing that it will be in service to us forever and taking for granted what a blessing it is to simply be alive.

Every day, our Physical Well is filled by movement, which means standing and moving throughout the day and not just working out for a set time once a day. It is also filled when we eat timely, balanced, and nutritious meals and drink water. And when we do so *before* we are so famished and weak that we feel like we are about to faint. Last, it is filled when we get adequate rest at night as opposed to pushing ourselves until we pass out from sheer exhaustion.

Our Physical Well is drained when we fail to incorporate regular and consistent movement throughout the day, get proper nutrition, and sleep seven hours or more each day.[5] And when our Physical Well is drained, it is nearly impossible for our other Personal Wells to function at optimal levels.

The Emotional Well

The Emotional Well is representative of our feelings and range of emotions, which, according to researchers at UC Berkeley, encompasses the following twenty-seven categories of emotions: admiration, adoration, aesthetic appreciation, amusement, anger, anxiety, awe, awkwardness, boredom, calmness, confusion, craving, disgust, empathic pain, entrancement, excitement, fear, horror, interest, joy, nostalgia, relief, romance, sadness, satisfaction, sexual desire, and surprise.[6] If you feel (no pun intended) like humans might have a greater emotional range than that, you are not alone. Psychologist Robert Plutchik believes humans can experience more than 34,000 emotions![7]

Every day, our Emotional Well is filled when we take the time to understand, manage, process, and express our emotions, which is not always easy. It is one of the reasons our Emotional Well can play a critical role in our lives of the most: Our emotions have a way of guiding our decisions, and they often govern whether we say yes to a request, even when we know we do not have the capacity.

Learning how to tend our Emotional Well is key to finding freedom from a life of overwhelm.

As you might imagine, our Emotional Well is easily drained by others. But we also drain it ourselves by not honestly expressing how we feel and instead using avoidance to escape, suppress, or repress our feelings.

The Mental Well

The Mental Well is representative of our brain and intellectual capacity. Every day, it is filled when we engage in activities that help us learn new ideas and information. This can be as simple as reading a book or more intensive, like attending engaging workshops at a conference. Our Mental Well is also filled when we engage in problem-solving that requires us to use the following skills:

- Identifying and understanding a problem.
- Examining and analyzing the problem.
- Brainstorming and creating possible solutions to the problem.
- Evaluating and assessing the likelihood of each solution's success.
- Taking action by implementing the solution to the problem.

Having strong problem-solving skills is crucial to resolving conflicts and overcoming challenges, but many people have not adequately developed these skills. Recent data shows that around 32 percent of US adults score below proficiency in adaptive problem-solving skills, meaning they struggle with solving even simple problems with few variables, indicating a significant portion of the population does not have strong problem-solving abilities.[8]

This also explains why people who do have strong problem-solving skills are constantly called upon for advice and support and tend to find themselves overwhelmed.

Our Mental Well is drained whenever we fail to prioritize fostering an environment that supports our mental awareness and intellectual growth. Our Mental Well is also drained when we forgo seeking professional therapy or counseling for challenges beyond our control.

The Social Well

The Social Well is representative of our interpersonal relationships. Every day, it is filled when we engage in healthy communication with our family, friends, and romantic partners. It is also filled when we receive support from our professional relationships, including former and current colleagues.

It is a historically and scientifically proven fact that humans do not fare well without the support of a community. We need one another to survive. Many of us experienced the truth of this firsthand during the pandemic. Even those of us who were lucky enough to have strong social bubbles lost access to the people who filled our Social Wells once our daily in-person interactions were limited. It is a truth that we are still in the process of grieving and healing.

The reason our Social Well is of particular importance is that it also allows us to fill our other Wells. For example, we can fill our Social *and* Emotional Wells when we meet up with a friend to share how we feel about a troubling issue. Likewise, we can fill our Social *and* Mental Wells when we work with a colleague to discuss a problem and brainstorm a solution. As you will later learn, when we are intentional about caring for our Social Well, we have the ability to fill *all* our Wells with one meetup or activity, which is pretty powerful.

Our Social Well is drained when we are unable to engage with our chosen community, when we fail to properly manage or support our interpersonal relationships, or when we tend to have more transactional connections and fewer genuine ones. And, of course, our Social Well is drained if we do not have a strong community or if we feel unsupported by the community in which we live and serve.

The Spiritual Well

It may seem that the Spiritual Well focuses solely on our religious practices, but it is more representative of our essence, of the soul of who we are. Depending on our belief system, our Spiritual Well can include and be filled by our religion or faith-based practices. However, on a universal level, it is filled when we believe that our work and contributions to the world are meaningful. Perhaps the most beautiful illustration of this concept is the Japanese word *ikigai*, which translates as "a reason for being."[9]

Ikigai is essentially our sweet spot, the merging of passion, talent, and fulfillment of one's purpose in life.[10] This sweet spot is not only sweet for you, but also encompasses something that the world needs, thereby allowing you to earn a living through your reason for being. For those of us fortunate enough to discover our *ikigai*, our Spiritual Well is filled with our work and day-to-day activities because we feel that what we are doing is meaningful. Of course, many people do not know their reason for being or may not believe they even have one. Nonetheless, the Spiritual Well is representative of the fulfillment (or emptiness) one feels throughout daily life.

For people who engage in religious, spiritual, or faith-based practices, staying connected to the source of those beliefs is integral to filling our Spiritual Well. Whether going to church or keeping an ancestral altar to those who have come before you, establishing consistent rituals and routines is key to ensuring this Well stays at an optimal level. It is drained whenever we feel disconnected from our grounding belief systems or feel that we are not living a meaningful life.

These Wells represent five core areas—our physical health, emotional health, mental health, social health, and spiritual health—that serve as the foundation for our wellness and well-being. However, I believe there is an additional area that we should consider when we do our self-assessment: our Historical Well. The inner work of finding freedom from a life of overwhelm requires us to identify and understand the beliefs and behaviors that cause us to take on more than we should or more than we have the capacity to manage. So, we need to get to the origin stories and experiences that have shaped and influenced us, many of which have been heavily influenced by the history of our lived experiences—personal, familial, cultural, and generational.

The Historical Well

The Historical Well is representative of our individual history, which is also comprised of our collective histories. It is filled when we actively engage in learning more about who we are holistically, based on our childhood, formative years, and adulthood as well as cultural and generational narratives that have been and remain influential in our everyday lives.

Our Historical Well is not just a Well that we tend to; it is a Well that we must dig in to because it essentially serves as the foundation for all our Wells—our Historical Well can reveal *why* we fill and drain the other Wells in the ways that we do. Excavating our Historical Well may explain:

- Why we neglect our Physical Well by forgoing daily movement, eating a balanced and nutritious diet, or getting adequate rest.
- Why we neglect our Emotional Well by avoiding, escaping, suppressing, or repressing our feelings.
- Why we neglect our Mental Well by forgoing engaging in activities that will increase our intellectual capacity or seeking professional care and counseling when we need it.
- Why we neglect our Social Well by choosing to be hyper-independent rather than seeking out meaningful connections and community.
- Why we neglect our Spiritual Well by abandoning our grounding belief systems or by forgoing opportunities to do meaningful work.

Our Historical Well is a powerful source of information, from which we can understand how we came to form the limiting beliefs that are preventing us from living the lives we want and deserve.

And what is even more special? Often, we are the first in our lineage to spend some time there.

A LOVE NOTE TO BLACK WOMEN

On Being the First . . .

It is believed that Mary Jane Patterson was the first Black woman to graduate from a US college in 1862 with a bachelor's degree from Oberlin College.[11] While few details are known about her family background, it is noted that she was the daughter of an enslaved person.[12] What *is* noted in detail is her determination to make history.

Unlike many colleges, Oberlin admitted not only African Americans but also women. Black students had graduated from the school, but without a four-year collegiate bachelor's degree. Patterson changed that. And, though Oberlin offered a two-year course for women, she insisted on taking the "gentleman's course" of study. At the time, women were not expected to immerse themselves in classical languages, mathematics, or science, but Patterson bucked the trend and took her place next to a class of white males. She held her own. When she graduated in 1862, it was with high honors.[13]

It is not uncommon for Black women to carry the weight of expected exceptionalism. And few expectations are as heavy as being "the first." The term "first generation" is often used in the context of educational achievements (e.g., first generation college student or graduate). But many Black women are also the first in our families to accomplish other meaningful milestones. We may be the first in our family to

- seek therapy and counseling.
- get a psychiatric diagnosis (and take the prescribed meds!).
- be in a healthy, committed relationship or be intentionally single.
- focus on healthy parenting or co-parenting relationships.
- not live paycheck to paycheck.
- invest and build wealth.

Many Black women are first generation cycle breakers in nearly every area of our lives.

Being first generation in ways that change the trajectory of our lineage is indeed something to celebrate . . . but it is also complicated. We worked hard. We made personal sacrifices. We stayed the course. We made it!

But now what?

Once we prove we are exceptional, what are we supposed to do *now*?

Often, we don't know what to do. So we just keep doing what we've always done: the most.

Yes, being first-gen is an accomplishment and it is also a unique lived experience: No one in your family can serve as a model for how to navigate your achievements. First-gen means being the first to battle the guilt of wanting to say no to opportunities that others may see as blessings. It means being the first to feel the pressures of personal responsibilities that come with success—being others' educators, translators, administrators, and financial advisers (and donors)—all while trying to figure out who we are and how we feel about our new status. Being first-gen often means there is a limiting belief that you have to keep striving for the next best thing . . . but it is a race that is impossible to win because the bar is always moving.

As someone who is first-gen in many areas of my life, I know firsthand how Black women who share the same label often feel like we are winning . . . until our well-being is compromised and we realize just how much we've lost and what it has cost us.

Black women, please know our first-gen achievements are truly to be lauded, especially given the intersectional hurdles and barriers that we face. But nothing that we accomplish is worth our compromising our well-being—physically, mentally, emotionally, socially, and spiritually. Consider whether you may be harboring other limiting beliefs about being "the first" in your family and whether they cause you to overextend, overachieve, or overperform to your detriment . . . and liberate yourself by letting those false narratives go.

Please note that self-assessing our Personal Wells is not a replacement for medical care. Maintaining annual appointments with a health care professional and adhering to their guidance is essential to our well-being. Rather, consider using the Personal Wells framework as a check-in tool to ensure you are prioritizing your well-being over doing everything for everyone else. Of course, there will always be times when we have to make personal sacrifices. But these circumstances certainly feel less sacrificial when they are occasional rather than the norm. Last, the Personal Wells framework is another way to discover the "why" behind your limiting beliefs. Because self-assessment and self-inquiry are like cousins: they both lead to self-awareness.

Remember, there is a price our bodies pay when we neglect our physical health. A price our minds pay when we neglect our mental and emotional health. A price our self-esteem and self-worth pay when we are not in alignment and in right relation with our family and friends. And a price to pay when we neglect our spiritual well-being for so long that we lose sight of our goals and purpose.

Remember, there is nothing more costly than being unwell.

FREEDOM FROM, FREEDOM FOR

Every so often, I still laugh about the time I went to the internet in search of advice on how to disappear. Apparently, I was seeking freedom long before I became the Afrominimalist! Seriously, these days, I know just how common it is for people to want freedom from their everyday lives. However, we tend to not be fully aware or specific enough about what we are seeking freedom *from*. Likewise, beyond having more time to and for ourselves, we may not give much thought to the life we are seeking freedom *for*.

Which is perhaps the reason why we often struggle with personal liberation: We don't know what we're escaping from or where we're going if we do get free.

Freedom From, Freedom For is a concept that encourages us to think more critically about liberation. It is not enough to simply want to be free from a life of overwhelm—we have to be intentional about what aspects of our lives we are freeing ourselves from, and just as importantly, what we're freeing ourselves for. Whether it's freedom from the limiting beliefs that are the source of our burnout, perfectionism, people-pleasing, or something more tangible, we must be willing to name what we want to release. Otherwise, we risk unknowingly recreating our troubles in new forms or even renaming them.

Perhaps what is best about the Freedom From/Freedom For concept is that you don't have to wait to give thought to the life you are seeking freedom for. In fact, you shouldn't wait! Because freedom isn't just about escape—it is equally about expansion. And here is the rub: Unless you have plans for your newfound freedom, you won't stay free from overwhelm for very long.

Early in my journey to finding freedom from my life of overwhelm, my sole focus was on doing what I needed to do to get well. And I did it! I quit the stressful job that caused my high blood pressure. I did the work of honoring myself by getting to know my limiting beliefs. And I spent time creating new liberating beliefs about myself and my self-worth.

Every day, every single day, I tended to my Personal Wells. And I refused to feel guilty for saying no to anyone and anything that did not align with the new woman I was slowly rediscovering and becoming. For the first time in my life, I prioritized my well-being over everyone and everything else. But not once did I think about what was next.

I probably would have continued on the path of being hyper-focused on being healthy and whole had it not been for an invitation that I received to attend a small group visioning class.

At the time, I was digging deeper into my Spiritual and Historical Wells, and I was in the early stages of building my first ancestral altar dedicated to honoring my lineage. The invitation to attend a visioning class seemed right on brand with other moments of synchronicity I'd experienced throughout my season of separation.

Somehow, I was always receiving exactly what I needed exactly when I was ready to receive it.

As soon as I walked into the Wellness House at Eaton Hotel, I felt a flood of emotions. During the pandemic, Eaton had been my second home, a haven. As local writers, two dear friends and I had been offered office space at an extreme discount. Ultimately, we ended up having the entire floor to ourselves.

Day after day, night after night, we worked on our projects in isolation but as together as we could be. We ventured into one another's offices with our masks on to workshop our books, share a meal, laugh, and vent, and also to cry. I'd written *The Afrominimalist's Guide to Living with Less* in that office. I'd been sitting in that office when I'd lovingly admonished one writer friend about online dating during the pandemic; she was now married to a person she'd met online. And I'd been sitting in that office when the other writer stood in the doorway, the appropriate social distance from my desk, and told me his father had just died. I hadn't even been able to hug him, only express my sympathies and sob once he was on the elevator and out of earshot.

What an unprecedented time indeed.

Now, as I laid my mat on the floor with a handful of other participants—some of us masked because we were still somewhat cautious, some unmasked (and I won't lie, it was nice to see full faces and smiles)—I could not help but wonder what such a class might have been like pre-pandemic. Of the life I might have envisioned for myself before spending that time in a state of overwhelm coupled with the unspoken grief of survivor's guilt.

Focus on being present, I reminded myself. *You are not the only person dealing with a past that you cannot change.*

The calming scent of palo santo swirled throughout the large, open space as we settled onto our mats and meditation pillows. I began to relax, leaning into my new liberating belief that I could just be a student in the class. I did not have to volunteer to help or share what little I knew about visioning. And I felt triumphant every time I successfully silenced the people pleaser in me.

There was nothing profound about the prompt the instructor gave—envision having a meeting with your future Self. And so I closed my eyes, eager to meet the silver fox I hoped to become someday.

In my dreamlike state, I found myself in a beautiful desert landscape, the sky cloudless and bright blue against the backdrop of what appeared to be red sandstone mountains. Initially, I was taken aback by this setting, surprised that my future Self had decided to live in what appeared to be New Mexico or Arizona (which of course I now know could also very well be Morocco!). Wherever I was, it was absolutely stunning. And so peaceful! I smiled, proud of my future Self for having followed through on my plans to one day escape the noisy hustle and bustle of city life.

I looked down at the pebbled pathway where I was standing, my eyes slowly following the walkway that led to a simple yet stunning adobe house. Painted a warm terra-cotta, the ranch-style dwelling reflected the surrounding earthen elements. As I walked toward the entrance, I took in the stillness, the serenity. There was literally no sound save for the soft crunch of gravel beneath my feet.

Beveled glass panels framed two large ebony wood double doors, and again I smiled. Because all of it was giving leisure and luxury.

Yes, ma'am! Looks like you did all right for yourself!

Carefully, I lifted the wrought-iron ring and rapped it against the door three times. Instantly, both doors opened in a slow, deliberate sweep, in perfect unison like the opening of a grand stage. And there was my future Self, standing there as if she had been awaiting my arrival.

My hair still in a buzz cut, only now all white. The smooth skin on my brow a bit more mature, my brown eyes a bit wiser. My bare feet, my toes polished in my favorite color—black—peeked out from the hem of a colorful caftan. The most prominent color in the dress's bright, bold pattern was turquoise, the same color as the smallest squares in the center of the floor's black ceramic tiles.

Wow. She is—I am—stunning!

I just stood there, staring at my future Self, smiling and spellbound. I mean, I'd always hoped I'd age well, but this was certainly more than I'd ever bargained for.

From the front door, I could see the interior's decor was meticulous. An open dining room centered by an ebony wood rectangular table with matching benches on either side. A living room off to the right, another room (was that my writing room?) off to the left. Glass patio doors leading out to a lush green backyard where the aqua blue of a swimming pool reflected the shining sun.

I could not stop staring at my future Self, smiling. And she too grinned at me, with equal love and admiration.

Just, wow. I can't wait to be you*!*

Bells began to chime, the soft ringing gently ushering our small class back into present-day consciousness. Everyone seemed just as excited as I was. We had all met our future Selves, and we were all eager to share our experiences. Thankfully, I went first. Because if I hadn't, I might not have had the courage to share after hearing of others' encounters.

One fellow classmate had tea with his future Self as they chatted about how their hardest moments in life had been necessary for their evolution. Another was proud to report that her future Self had a conversation in the very home that she and her husband hoped to one day build. Another woman had argued with her future Self, a silly disagreement to inform her that yes, she'd continue her love of debating well into old age.

I was the only person who hadn't engaged with her future Self. She hadn't even said two words to me let alone invited me inside *our* future home! Now I wasn't sure about the grin that seemed so sweet. Now, it seemed more akin to "Silly girl. You are not ready to come into this house and hear what I have to say."

I was crushed.

For the next several days, I ruminated on that vision session. I could not stop thinking about the one common thread in my classmates' reflections: They all had things to discuss with their future Selves. Meanwhile, I was just in awe to see my future Self and, if I'm honest, I was just happy that she—we—had survived. It was sobering to realize that I'd spent so many years stuck on autopilot, that I'd spent so much time going and doing, just trudging through one overwhelming day at a time, that I hadn't given much to my future Self beyond hoping she'd be a silver fox.

I was so focused on seeking freedom that I had not given much thought to what my life would look and feel like once I found it, which was likely the reason I *hadn't* found it—I had nothing to turn my compass toward beyond getting through my daily to-do list.

Sometimes, most times, we need to be pushed off course from living our lives on autopilot. Forced to stop doing what feels comfortable even though it no longer comforts and feeds our souls. Forced to stop doing what feels safe even though the mundaneness threatens our sanity. Forced to stop going with the flow of a tide that never wavers enough to challenge or strengthen us in any way. Sometimes, most times, we need something to make us hungry, especially when our bellies have been full for so long.

Sometimes, we need our future Selves to make us pause and take a long, hard look at how we are living our present lives.

SPEND A DAY IN THE LIFE YOU'RE SEEKING FREEDOM FOR

The following prompts are designed to help you envision spending a day with your future Self. And I want you to spend it in the life you are seeking freedom for. Whether you write out your answers or create a vision board, the goal and purpose is for you to give serious thought to the life you want and deserve.

- **Where do you live?** Name the city, state, or country. Describe your home at sunrise.
- **Who wakes up by your side?** Describe your current partner, ideal future partner, or whether you are single by choice.
- **How do you start your day?** Describe your morning routine.
- **When do you start working and what are you working on?** Describe what it looks and feels like when you are working on regular ol' Monday (remember: *ikigai*!).
- **When you chat with dear friends for lunch, how do you tell them about your weekend?** Describe where you went or what you made for lunch, what you did, and who, if anyone, was with you.
- **How do you spend your afternoon?** Describe your afternoon routine, whether it involves taking a nap, getting back to work, attending a class, or spending time alone or with loved ones.
- **What are your dinner plans?** Describe where you went or what you made for dinner (or if someone made dinner for you!), where you're going (even if it is only to your dining room), what you're wearing, and whether you have company.

- **How do you wind down for the evening?** Describe your evening routine, whether it is drawing a bath, taking a long shower, or doing a bit of yoga.
- **How do you close out your day?** Describe your perfect nighttime routine before you drift off to sleep.

Now that you know the life you are seeking freedom from and have given serious thought to the life you are seeking freedom for, it is time to officially embark upon your journey to liberation. You will soon learn what is necessary to let go of the limiting beliefs that no longer serve you. Because although liberation sounds lovely, it is indeed work. And there are aspects of that work that are nonnegotiable. But please know that every step of your journey is worth it, that every milestone yields its own reward. Mine led me to five words that have become one of my favorite mantras: Healing is worth the work.

May you be encouraged as you do what is necessary to find freedom from your life of overwhelm. And may you be excited as you take the first steps toward the life you are seeking freedom for; one where you are in alignment with what you believe in, want, and deserve. And, of course, a life where you are well—physically, mentally, emotionally, socially, and spiritually.

CHAPTER 3

THE JOURNEY OF LIBERATION

Congratulations on making the commitment to honor yourself. It is the work of personal transformation that leads to personal liberation. It begins the moment you choose to listen to your needs, trust your intuition, and stop betraying yourself for the sake of being accepted, admired, or approved. Freedom is the work of selfishly, unapologetically choosing ourselves time and time again.

Whether you know it or not, you have already made great strides to prepare for your journey ahead. You have a better understanding of overwhelm. You are more aware of your limiting beliefs and know how they influence your choices. You know how to use the Personal Wells framework to self-assess your capacity and well-being. So please know that you have not only taken the first steps away from the life you are seeking freedom from but also you have begun to walk boldly toward the life you are seeking freedom for.

Now it is time to take everything you have learned thus far and begin implementing these practices into your life with intention.

It is important to note that the road to liberation is not one to be traveled quickly. Moving with intention does not mean rushing to do the inner work or making hasty decisions. Yes, you have a longing to be free, but honoring that longing will require you to move slowly and deliberately. Embedded in every facet of freedom is the need to be strategic and steadfast in our choices, which is impossible to do without giving the decisions we make careful thought and consideration. Learning to pause is a muscle that you must learn to strengthen for you to both get free *and* stay free from overwhelm.

Many of us only know of liberation in the collective sense:

> "Until we are all free, we are none of us free."
> —Emma Lazarus

This powerful quote was penned by Emma Lazarus, a late nineteenth-century American poet and activist, to address antisemitism.[1] There have since been many iterations that speak to the interconnectedness of freedom and social movements. From Fannie Lou Hamer to Martin Luther King Jr., we've been conditioned to see freedom as a shared struggle, not a personal journey. Without a doubt, while collective liberation *is* indeed important, it differs greatly from our personal freedom.

> Our personal freedom is composed of the individual rights, choices, and internal shifts that allow us to live in alignment with our values, needs, and truth. Being free means no longer being beholden to beliefs, behaviors, and expectations that no longer serve us.

When we seek personal liberation, we are committing to the process of being introspective to discover our limiting beliefs and getting to the root of our "why." We are agreeing to let go of identities that no longer serve us, and welcoming the act of surrendering to the cycle of grieving who we were and what it cost us. We are choosing to come into alignment with who we are now as well as be protective about who we are becoming.

The journey of personal liberation is the inner work of lovingly self-assessing our beliefs and behaviors, not to critique but to change and become the next best version of ourselves.

THE INNER WORK

When I began writing the first draft of *Less Is Liberation*—which, unbeknownst to me, was the start of *my* journey to personal freedom—I had no idea it would lead to me spending more than a year immersed in being introspective. Sure, I knew I'd have to (*and* I wanted to) get to know myself a bit more, but I had no idea I'd need to get *so* up close and personal with my thoughts and feelings. I had no idea how uncomfortable it would be to interrogate myself nor how utterly embarrassed, hurt, and disappointed I'd be when reflecting on my past. I had no idea that the journey of liberation was less about doing something and more about being still.

So again, let me reiterate that the journey of learning how to honor yourself cannot and should not be rushed. Having been through the process myself, I know that it is much easier said than done. The moment we start to see how much our limiting beliefs and life of overwhelm have already cost, it is so incredibly tempting to start course correcting immediately. Which is why I created a road map—the necessities—to help you stay focused on the inner work required for your Freedom From/ Freedom For journey. Out of all the twists and turns I made to liberate myself from the beliefs, behaviors, and expectations that no longer served me, the four necessities that I share here are what I kept returning to time and time again. In fact, I still use them whenever I find myself being tempted to resort to old patterns or behaviors. Perhaps you will find it easy to think of them as mile markers as you move forward.

MILE MARKERS TO PERSONAL LIBERATION

Now that you know the interconnectedness between overwhelm and our overall well-being, it should come as no surprise that the four necessities focus primarily on the Personal Wells framework. Each mile marker is designed to guide you through the inner work of your liberatory journey by teaching you how to honor yourself honestly and holistically.

Mile Marker #1: Assess the Wells

Your journey will begin with a full self-assessment of your Personal Wells. This will require you to do a few things you may not have done in a while. Spend some time in solitude. Take a purposeful pause. Allow yourself to be introspective without judgment. The purpose of this assessment is to discover the limiting beliefs you are seeking freedom from and the identities that do not align with the life you are seeking freedom for.

Mile Marker #2: Heal the Wells

Being able to identify the limiting beliefs, behaviors, and identities that keep us trapped in a cycle of overwhelm is so empowering. And it is here at this second mile marker that you will learn to let them go. Healing our Wells requires us to release what no longer serves us and surrender to the inevitable grief. Because even though you must say goodbye to those versions of yourself that no longer align with your highest good, they are still a part of the story of you. It is not uncommon to have to return to this mile marker time and time again. Remember, healing is worth the work.

Mile Marker #3: Protect the Wells

Once we do the work to heal our Personal Wells, it is our responsibility to ensure we keep them from being depleted, especially as we prepare to take our first official steps into the life we are seeking freedom for. At this mile marker, you will learn how to use your superpower: your ability to choose to prioritize your well-being selfishly and unapologetically. It is here that you will establish your terms for liberation; terms that will govern how you enjoy and maintain the life you've been seeking freedom for.

Mile Marker #4: Fill the Wells

There are aspects of each mile marker that I love, but this last one is perhaps my favorite because it is the celebratory mile marker! The one where you are officially liberated from your overwhelming life of doing! You have done the necessary inner work to come into alignment with the life you want and deserve. Being intentional about filling your Personal Wells is how you sustain your liberated life. At this mile marker, I share some of my favorite rituals and routines to keep you grounded in the ten facets of freedom.

This is a journey, *your* journey. Not a journey *to* someplace, but rather a journey *of* becoming someone new.

While the necessities lead us to personal liberation, what we experience on our respective journeys will be unique. For example, what I found most challenging, and even still struggle to forgive, is how much of my life I'd spent abandoning and neglecting myself.

Although it has gotten easier to accept, I still have moments when I reflect on how I did not have time to care for myself because I was constantly helping and caring for others. I did not have the energy to devote to my health because I was constantly depleted from being in service to others. And even though I hate to admit it, there is also evidence that I spent much of my life loving others more than I loved myself.

Love is a multifaceted emotion, and it requires connection and commitment. That is what is hardest for me to accept—that I spent so much of my life being disconnected and uncommitted to myself.

I share these painful acknowledgments to be honest about the journey to personal liberation. Much of the process is nothing like the beautiful, commercialized, and commodified version of self-care that we are accustomed to seeing. I want you to know that, yes, your journey will have many beautiful moments of clarity and change. And also, there will be aspects that are hard for you to hold and accept as true.

As you learn to take agency over your life, phrases like "and also" will become commonplace. Agency is the ability to name our truths, make intentional choices, and respond to life in ways that align with who we are—not who we were taught or think we have to be to please others. You will learn to hold multiple truths with compassion:

I am so grateful. And also, I am tired.
I am so strong. And also, I need support.
I am setting boundaries. And also, I am learning not to feel guilty.

Taking agency over our lives is how we start to reclaim truths we once silenced or dismissed. It means deciding what kind of life we want to create with what we've been given. Agency is what it means to move beyond survival and into sovereignty.

Because our lives will never change unless we do.

THE OTHER WORK

By now I'm sure you are eager to start your journey. But there is one final consideration before you begin. It is what I like to call the "other work," which is the practice of being patient and extending ourselves compassion. Here is how the inner work and the other work complement each other:

> The inner work of personal liberation helps us discover what we need to change. The other work helps us stay the course when the process is difficult or change takes time.

While other work is often overlooked, it is equally as necessary as inner work. Let it serve as a gentle reminder that you don't have to fix everything at once. Other work is learning to rest without guilt, to give yourself grace when old patterns resurface, to celebrate progress even when it feels small. This is the work of being with yourself—not just pushing through. Without patience and compassion, even the most profound insights from the inner work can turn into new forms of pressure and perfectionism. But when you give yourself permission to move slowly, to feel deeply, and to heal on your own timeline, you create the safety and self-trust needed for lasting change. That is what the other work is really about: learning to hold space for who you're becoming.

A LOVE NOTE TO BLACK WOMEN

You Deserve to Be Free. You Deserve to Be Well.

Although I have no statistical evidence, I stand by a lifetime of personal and professional lived experiences: Black women, more than any other demographic, have normalized living in a constant state of overwhelm, which means Black women are more likely to be unwell. We are constantly being depleted, and we rarely allow ourselves the time and space to rest and recharge. We push through. We keep going. We carry it all. Masking our overwhelm or wearing it as a badge of honor. Until.

I know it is hard to read these truths and even harder to accept them. But as the old folks say, "It's the truth anyhow." Black women's overall health is constantly at risk. And we deserve better. We deserve to be well. But the only way we will get well is by prioritizing being well. And the only way we can stay well is by committing to change.

No matter how challenging or uncomfortable, we must commit to unlearning limiting beliefs that our worth is measured by how much we endure, how much we give, or how little we need others. It starts with one decision: to put ourselves first. Wellness is our birthright. And it's time we reclaim it.

Much of the guidance I share in *Less Is Liberation* is intuitive wisdom—our bodies know what we need to be well. And as I discovered during my season of being unable to force myself to do anything, our bodies are always trying to get well. Put simply, this book is

designed to provide the tools, language, and framework to remind you to listen to and trust what your whole being is telling you when it is time for you to take care of yourself. In doing so, you will undoubtedly discover the overwhelming life you are seeking freedom from can actually be a catalyst for pursuing the life you are seeking freedom for: one of optimal wellness.

PART II

THE NECESSITIES

REVISITING OUR PERSONAL WELLS

Before you move forward on your journey to Personal Liberation, let's return—gently and intentionally—to your Personal Wells. Earlier, you were invited to imagine yourself as a vessel, filled and sustained by these vital areas of your health. Now, as you prepare to do the deeper inner work required to find freedom from your life of overwhelm, it is essential to revisit the Personal Wells framework to reinforce your understanding of what each "Well" entails. Your Personal Wells are the foundation of honoring and prioritizing your overall well-being.

The Physical Well

This Well is representative of our body. Our Physical Well is filled when we engage our body in physical activity; eat timely, balanced, and nutritious meals; hydrate with water; and get adequate rest.

The Emotional Well

This Well is representative of our feelings. Our Emotional Well is filled whenever we allow ourselves to understand, manage, process, and convey how we feel.

The Mental Well

This Well is representative of our brain and intellectual capacity. Our Mental Well is filled whenever we engage in activities that help us learn new ideas and information, such as reading and engaging in other forms of educational media.

The Social Well

This Well is representative of our interpersonal relationships—familial, romantic, platonic, and professional. Our Social Well is our village, and it is filled whenever we engage in healthy communication and maintain supportive connections.

The Spiritual Well

This Well represents more than our religious beliefs and denomination. Our Spiritual Well represents our essence—it is the soul of who we are—and it is at its optimal level when we believe that our work and contributions to the world are meaningful.

The Historical Well

This is a bonus Well, one that I found useful to add. It is not only representative of our past but is also comprised of our collective histories. Our Historical Well teaches us more about who we are holistically, and it requires us to explore our childhood, formative years, and adulthood as well as any influential cultural and generational narratives.

CHAPTER 4

ASSESS THE WELLS

Although my trip to Morocco ultimately led me to acknowledge and understand personal freedom, it most certainly did not start in a liberating way. In fact, it started with me standing in line at Royal Air Maroc wondering if I'd made the right decision. Now that I was familiar with the telltale signs of hypertension, I knew that my dizziness and blurring vision meant my blood pressure was rising, even though I had taken my medication. And I knew it was because I was stressed.

As the trip and my editorial deadline neared, I'd spent less time writing and more time ruminating on my past. I'd spent day after day, week after week, being introspective to the point of making myself depressed. I'd long since passed self-assessing my Personal Wells for the purposes of understanding what beliefs led to my self-neglecting behaviors—I was in full-on self-critique mode, constantly berating myself. Now that I'd done the inner work, I could see clearly just how much my people-pleasing had drained my time and energy over the years.

Yes, I was on the mend, having just started to take my health seriously. But all the incessant ruminating seemed to be counterproductive, making me feel more unwell. And it all came to a head that afternoon as I stood in line, waiting to check in to my flight to Morocco. To be honest, I was afraid that if I looked anything near how I felt, I might not be allowed to board. My vision blurred, which I now knew was a sign that my blood pressure was high.

Breathe, Christine. Breathe.

Smiling, I handed my passport to the agent and muttered something about being excited for my first visit to North Africa. Thankfully, whatever I said worked. I had no idea that I was embarking on a journey where I would learn more about my wellness and, no pun intended, about actual wells.

The flight was uneventful—or rather, if anything eventful had happened, I certainly missed it. I slept the entire trip, and I continued resting after I arrived in Casablanca and settled into my hotel.

Early the next morning, as I joined the other guests for our first excursion, I felt none of the stress I'd felt less than twenty-four hours before. I'd eaten a delicious, healthy dinner and drank more Moroccan mint tea than any one person should consume—it was just so good! I'd also spent the night with my windows open, sleeping to the sound of ocean waves gently lapping against the shore. Smiling, I remembered Dr. G's wisdom: Our bodies are always, *always* trying to be well.

It hadn't even taken a full day for my body to recover. I was glad I'd listened and allowed it to do what it needed to do.

Our first destination was the Atlas Mountains, and it took several hours to drive there. I spent much of that time looking out the window and daydreaming as the traditional Berber music softly playing through the truck's speakers lulled me into an occasional nap. I looked forward to seeing the mountains, but the adventure I was most excited about was still a few days away: exploring the Sahara Desert.

By the time we arrived at the desert town of Erfoud, I felt like a new woman. Being in nature, being in good company, being in towns where every meal was farm-to-table, had calmed my nervous system and my soul. Whenever I pulled out my leather-bound journal to write, the words seemed to pour onto the page, which was in stark contrast to the writer's block I'd been experiencing for months. And my rest! Every night I had the most peaceful, easeful rest in riads nestled under the stars.

Slowly but surely, I was getting well. And now that I knew what wellness felt like, now that overwhelm was no longer my baseline, I had a better understanding of just how stressed I'd been over the past year. The difference was so stark that, honestly, it was frightening. But I also knew I would never again embody that state of being. Nothing and no one was worth compromising my overall well-being.

Our journey to Erfoud would be short, but for me, it would be the most meaningful educational destination on the trip for one reason: I would learn about the origins and intricacies of well systems, *khettaras*, that were used thousands of years ago to bring water from the distant mountains to desert towns below.

Averaging twelve to eighteen miles in length, these ancient irrigation systems are no longer in use. But visitors can walk through the old tunnel systems with guides who explain how they once worked—very much like how our bodies work. When observed from the outside, above ground, these intricate systems do not look like much at all. In fact, there is no aboveground structure similar to the circular brick channels with buckets that we are so accustomed to associating with well systems. Rather, on the surface, the well systems look like several molehills scattered throughout the desert. It is only once you go below the surface that you discover how intricately complex and beautiful they are.

In ancient times, each tribe was responsible for maintaining a section of the irrigation system, which required them to upkeep several wells. It was necessary to care for these wells similarly to the way we need to maintain our Personal Wells: by routinely checking and *assessing* each well to see if anything needs to be cleaned and cleared. Making structural repairs to *heal* the wells to prevent further damage. *Protecting* the wells because they are so crucial to our survival. Periodically doing so is the only way to ensure that our wells stay as *filled* as possible, which is why taking time to pause and assess your Personal Wells is the first necessity.

Because we *know* when we are doing the most. We see it in our inability to differentiate when we are *at* capacity versus when we have *surpassed* our capacity. We hear it in our conversations. In fact, we don't even mind telling others how we're feeling:

"I am so swamped."
"I am under so much pressure."
"I am stretched so thin."
"I am struggling to keep up."
"I am drowning."
"I am drained."
"It's just all too much right now."

Yet it seems that nothing we see or hear is enough to make us heed the warnings our bodies are trying to show and tell us. We never stop! We won't even pause long enough to ask ourselves one simple question: Why?

Much like the keepers of the ancient Moroccan *khettaras*, we must regularly inspect ourselves to discover the source of our overwhelm and understand how it is impacting our well-being. Although this can certainly be done under the care of a health professional (and should be done during your annual checkup), we should also learn how to check in with ourselves moment by moment, day by day. Because no one spends more time with you than you. So let's begin the beautiful work of being intentional about the time you spend alone.

THE NECESSITY OF SOLITUDE

> "But many of us seek community solely to escape the fear of being alone. Knowing how to be solitary is central to the art of loving. When we can be alone, we can be with others without using them as a means of escape."—bell hooks, *All About Love: New Visions*

I know what you might be thinking:

Bring on the solitude! I love being alone!

Anyone who has ever experienced overwhelm knows the longing to be alone, if only to have the chance to rest and recharge. There have likely been many times when you sought alone time as a respite or even as a reward for all your hard work. But there is a difference between being alone and seeking solitude for the purpose of personal liberation.

Even those of us who are self-proclaimed loners are biologically wired to seek comfort, safety, and security with others. We know that being in community has and always will be integral to human survival. However, we were never meant to be in constant contact and communication with others, and most certainly not at the level of accessibility and accountability modern technology allows.

In our professional lives, the use of email and team-centered communication apps and platforms blurs the line between the start and end of the workday. In our personal lives, the use of social media blurs the line between genuine friendships and transactional relationships. Not to mention being accessible through DMs and accountable to answer questions and comments or, even worse, publicly defend ourselves. So, although we have moments when we are physically alone, rarely are we truly mentally, emotionally, and socially alone.

That is why solitude is necessary for your personal liberation: so that you may come to know and trust yourself more intimately. Consider this moment a sacred time to take a purposeful pause from your life of overwhelm.

Pausing does not require us to retreat to the mountains or spend hours deep in meditation. All that is required is an intentional moment of stillness. No phone. No distractions. Just you . . . sitting with yourself . . . in silence.

Often, we struggle with pausing for the same reason we struggle with solitude: Being with ourselves can be very confronting. Without distractions, we have no choice but to face the thoughts, emotions, and truths we have been avoiding. This is the inner work required for personal liberation. Because only when we stop going and doing the most do we finally have the time and space to honor ourselves by thinking critically about who we were, who we are, and who we are becoming.

A LOVE NOTE TO BLACK WOMEN

Take a Purposeful Pause

One thing about Black women, we stay ready to do something, *anything* that empowers and enriches our lives. Rarely do we pause, not even to mourn our losses.

Instead, we pride ourselves on shaking off defeat and making more moves. While our "ain't nothing gonna keep me down" attitude is commendable at times, it is equally important that we allow ourselves to be comfortable with taking a purposeful pause.

We come from a long history of believing our worth is measured in how hard we work and what we bring to the table. We were taught to not be idle, to not be lazy, and to not waste our time. Whether we were conditioned by our community or by grind culture, we tend to believe that if we pause, we are *thisclose* to stopping. And if we stop—even for a moment—we are *thisclose* to falling behind. And if we fall behind, we will never catch up.

We have never been taught that pausing can be purposeful.

We have never been told that the time we enjoy wasting is not wasted time.*

Make no mistake, pausing *can* feel uncomfortable . . . at first. Because stillness forces us to sit with our thoughts, emotions, and uncertainties—things we often avoid. Things that are of the utmost importance for us to address if we want to be well. You will find yourself trying to answer the question: What am I supposed to be doing?

But perhaps, in that stillness, the real question that needs answering is: Who am I becoming?

So, take a purposeful pause.

It is a necessity on your journey of learning to honor yourself and your longing to be free.

---

* The quote "The time you enjoy wasting is not wasted time" is often attributed to Bertrand Russell, but it has also been attributed to Marthe Troly-Curtin and John Lennon.

Solitude is sacred. Just being alone is invitation in and of itself to be introspective. In the quiet, we begin to see ourselves more clearly—our thoughts, our patterns, our deeply held beliefs. Without the noise of outside expectations, we're able to gently examine the stories we've inherited and the assumptions we've internalized. Solitude gives us the space to ask, *Why do I feel the need to keep going when I'm exhausted? Why do I believe that going out of my way for others is the only way they'll love and respect me?*

The questions we ask ourselves are not always easy to answer. But self-inquiry is necessary nonetheless. Because at the core of any decision to neglect ourselves is a limiting belief that no longer serves us. And asking ourselves why is where introspection begins.

THE NECESSITY OF INTROSPECTION

When I began writing *The Afrominimalist's Guide to Living with Less*, I was already five years into my transition from being an overconsuming maximalist to becoming a rather unconventional minimalist. I had already struggled through the emotional labor of "letting go," so I felt confident providing guidance to help others understand their motivations and sever their attachments to things. I had also already completed the physical labor of "letting go," so I felt comfortable sharing a holistic process that incorporated forgiveness and encouraged taking a "need, use, love" approach to release things that no longer serve us.

Writing *The Afrominimalist's Guide* was sweet because *I* was in a sweet spot.

I was still close enough to revisit the difficulties I'd faced in my decision to live with less. Still able to recall how I'd overcome each challenge without compromising my authenticity. Writing about the experience was actually cathartic. I'd come so far from having fifty-two pairs of jeans and sixty-four pairs of shoes! From loading my first donation bag to giving my first TEDx talk, I truly enjoyed being a minimalist—the Afrominimalist, thank you very much—and writing about my experience through the lens of reflection.

Chronicling *Less Is Liberation* was different.

Very different.

It wasn't difficult to write about the overwhelm itself—sharing my thoughts about *that* feeling was certainly my wheelhouse! The real challenge was deciding to go deeper, to not only address our general understanding but also consider its impact through the lens of wellness. I'd already had to face the uncomfortable truth that I was unwell not because of the pressures in my life but rather my decision to never pause long enough to give my body what it needed. I was in the thick of discovering and confronting the limiting beliefs that caused me to take on more at the expense of my health and sanity. Honestly, it was somewhat embarrassing—was I *ready* to share my journey to being well with the world?

My people-pleasing?

My fixation on being a fixer?

My pride in being seen as productive?

My overwhelm masquerading as a proud overachiever?

Intuitively, I knew it would be better to show the inner work of *being* introspective as well as provide instructive guidance on the process. Because let's just say that discovering the limiting *beliefs* that caused me to do the most to my own detriment made releasing *things* that no longer served me feel like child's play.

THE INNER WORK OF INTROSPECTION

Many people believe that being introspective is akin to meditation, that we need silence, stillness, and solitude to "tap into" our deepest thoughts and desires. But let me assure you that nothing could be further from the truth. Yes, introspection happens with intention. But it also happens at random. Because it is actually quite common to look at ourselves with curiosity (although we could do a better job of doing so through the lens of compassion!).

Introspection can happen anywhere and anytime and while you are in the midst of doing anything. Yes, *anything*.

Mid-conversation. While watching a television show or listening to a podcast that hits a little too on the mark. On your drive to the grocery store. As you walk the aisles at said grocery store. As the cashier asks a question and you stare at her blankly, unable to respond because you were zoned out. This is why taking a purposeful pause to be introspective is so important: It *ensures* you are intentional. Remember: We are responsible for our lives of overwhelm. And being introspective is where and how we discover why we need to let go and what we need to let go of:

What are the limiting beliefs that are quietly shaping our lives?

What are the stories that we are telling ourselves that no longer serve us?

What are the habits and patterns that we keep repeating that are hindering our progress?

Perhaps you have always believed that hard work is the price of success—so you push yourself past exhaustion, convinced that rest is only for those who have earned it.

Perhaps you have internalized the idea that other people's happiness matters more than your own—so you say yes when you want to say no, prioritize their comfort over your well-being, and feel guilty whenever you put yourself first.

Perhaps you fear that if you slow down you will fall behind. So you fill every moment with tasks, measure your worth by your productivity, and struggle to enjoy any success you achieve because you are already chasing the next goal.

Perhaps you have convinced yourself that it is safer to stay where you are, even if you are unhappy. So you remain in situations that drain you, believing that the discomfort of the unknown is worse than the pain of staying the same.

The work of introspection invites us to ask ourselves: Do my beliefs reflect who I am becoming or who I believe myself to be? The moment we begin questioning our limiting beliefs—challenging and unraveling them—is the moment we begin to set ourselves free.

A LOVE NOTE TO BLACK WOMEN

Introspection Invites Compassion, Not Critique, to Change

I know all too well what it means to be raised with the singular focus of survival. From a young age, Black women are often taught to do the inner work of introspection with very strict parameters:

To find our flaws.

To tend to aspects of ourselves where we need to tighten up.

To do better, to look better, to be better.

We are taught to look at ourselves through a lens of critique rather than compassion.

But please know that introspection is not a call to dissect yourself. It is an opportunity to discover yourself, to learn more about who you really are as opposed to who you have been told to be. It is an invitation to lovingly sit with yourself. Not to scrutinize but to softly, ever so softly, decipher between what is true and what is false.

The inner work of introspection is about looking within not to fix yourself but rather to find yourself.

The "you" without your limiting beliefs.

The "you" who doesn't comply with others' labels and expectations.

The "you" who is honoring her longing to be free.

Through the inner work of introspection, yes, we learn the hard things: how we allowed every unacknowledged limiting belief to become an invisible barrier. But we do so softly, ever so softly, with the understanding that our newfound awareness is not for critique or condemnation. Rather, it is for us to take action to change and move forward toward the lives we are seeking freedom for.

It is a necessity on your journey of learning to honor yourself and your longing to be free.

Introspection is like conducting a personal performance evaluation—you are both the reviewer *and* the one being reviewed. And just like in any effective evaluation, the goal is not to criticize but to understand. Being introspective is an honest self-assessment of how you have been showing up in your life; it should help you to discern the limiting beliefs and behaviors that have you in a state of misalignment.

Perhaps you already have a framework that guides you through the work of introspection. If not, consider conducting a Personal Wells Performance Evaluation using the following questionnaire that I created to assist in *my* inner work of introspection. You can sit with yourself, think about each reflection, and answer them silently. Or you can journal your answers to make sure you capture your thoughts. Approach self-assessment in whatever way works best for you.

Remember: Every choice we make is rooted in a belief. Our beliefs are the result of messages that were given to us by messengers we trusted. If a messenger gave us the wrong message, knowingly or unknowingly, we may have formed a limiting belief. Discover your limiting beliefs and you will discover the wrong messages that are governing your life and causing you to be out of alignment.

PERSONAL WELLS PERFORMANCE EVALUATION

A compassionate introspective check-in to self-assess your alignment.

Physical Well: *Am I tending to my body with rest, nourishment, and movement?*

- What messages have I internalized about rest and productivity?
- Am I listening to my body's signs and symptoms—or overriding them to meet external expectations?

Mental Well: *Are my thoughts mostly helpful or harmful?*

- What stories have been replaying in my mind lately?
- Are these thoughts supporting clarity and self-trust—or creating confusion and self-doubt?

Emotional Well: *Am I giving myself space to feel, process, and release?*

- Have I been honoring my feelings or trying to mute them?
- What feelings have I been afraid to name—and what might shift if I gave them my undivided attention?

Social Well: *Are my relationships energizing or exhausting?*

- Where am I over-giving, overexplaining, or overextending myself to be accepted?
- Who truly sees, supports, and respects me as I evolve—and who only enjoys being around me when I shrink?

Spiritual Well: *Am I staying connected to whatever grounds me?*

- What practices or rituals help me feel rooted, present, and whole in my personal and professional life?

- Am I creating space for gratitude—or have I become spiritually disconnected?

These inquiries are designed to help you go deeper to answer the most important question: Why?

We know the inner work of introspection will not be easy. We know it means asking the hard questions we have been avoiding and sitting with the discomfort of our answers. And also, we know that every time we pause to do so, we are choosing to honor ourselves. On the next page are a few additional ways to engage in introspection that can lead to clarity, growth, and lasting liberation.

Dedicate Time, Dedicate Space

Of course, we can't all take a week off from work to spend time in solitude being introspective (but if you have unused vacation or sick hours, this is the perfect reason to take leave!). Also, please know spending time in solitude for the purpose of being introspective is not a twenty-four-hour affair. Rather, it is as simple as dedicating time to doing the inner work—be it one hour or once a week for the next several months. Likewise, it is important to have a dedicated space or solo activity, such as going for a walk or meditating, that allows you to be with your thoughts uninterrupted.

Ask Questions, Ask More Questions

Without a doubt, acknowledging that I was living in a constant state of overwhelm was the easiest part of my journey—acknowledging the reasons why I always felt like I was unable to cope was indeed the most difficult because I had to go deep into my Historical Well. And each question I answered led to more questions.

Vulnerability and honesty are at the core of introspection. There is nothing more vulnerable than asking yourself questions that, when you answer honestly, will expose your limiting beliefs and behaviors.

Be Patient, Be Kind

Despite knowing we're all just trying to figure out this wild and wonderful adventure called life, we have a habit of being incredibly hard on ourselves instead of having compassion and giving ourselves grace. Introspection is a process, not a one-time event. Some realizations about your limiting beliefs and behaviors will come quickly. Others may be a slow unveiling. Approach each inquiry with curiosity and compassion. Know that each discovery can yield more discoveries, some of which may take time to come to fruition. Accept these truths as part of the introspective process, and remember to be patient with yourself.

Share a Little, Keep a Little

Sometimes introspection reveals wounds that require deeper healing. It is not uncommon to discover family secrets or generational trauma that requires the support and counseling of a professional. If and when this happens, consider taking the African American adage "share a little, keep a little" to heart. Whether you decide to work with a trusted therapist or seek spiritual guidance, it is to your advantage to seek out professional counsel on how to best proceed with sharing information with loved ones.

Commit to Change, Commit to Choose Less

One of the biggest benefits of introspection is that it can be transformative. Identifying our limiting beliefs and behaviors gives us such clarity when we self-assess our Personal Wells—we can pinpoint exactly how and know the reasons why we continue to find ourselves in a constant state of overwhelm. And once we pinpoint them, we can commit to choose less—a small but mighty step that allows us to immediately start changing our circumstances.

Think of introspection as a mirror, reflecting not just who we are today but also the beliefs, experiences, and narratives that have shaped us. Without this reflection, we risk living on autopilot, unaware of how much our past continues to influence our present. One of the most transformative aspects of introspection is its ability to help us identify and dismantle limiting beliefs. These beliefs often act as invisible chains, dictating our choices without us even realizing it.

Through introspection, you can trace these beliefs back to their origins—perhaps they were inherited from family, shaped by societal expectations, or rooted in past experiences.

Once you see them clearly, you can begin to rewrite them. Instead of believing that rest is laziness, you might adopt the belief that *rest is a revolutionary act of self-preservation.*

Introspection is a gift we give to ourselves—a chance to step off the hurried treadmill of life we create for ourselves and ask, Am I moving in the right direction?

The inner work of introspection is a practice, but please remember that it is not about perfection. The commitment to personal liberation means you are always a work-in-progress. You are committing to learn how to live with greater intention and authenticity—there's no place for perfectionism when we choose to honor ourselves this way. It is how we come into alignment with the lives we are seeking freedom for with more wisdom about who we are now and who we're becoming.

CHAPTER 5
HEAL THE WELLS

I have no doubt that assessing your Personal Wells has resulted in you having a lot of feels. Throughout the weeks leading up to the day I boarded my flight to Morocco, I felt so many emotions as I was forced to confront many uncomfortable truths about my past. And I did not feel better, nor could I get better until I allowed myself to acknowledge and experience the pain of what I'd lost and still needed to let go. I'd never be able to recoup the time, energy, and resources I'd poured into others. Even though I'd identified several limiting beliefs, as well as the identities they'd formed, I still needed to let them go.

I was struggling to forgive myself for putting others' needs before my own and staying in unhealthy dynamics—personal and professional—long past their expiration date.

I was ready to stop being a people pleaser while simultaneously struggling with how it might impact my interpersonal relationship. Even though I hated to admit it, I took pride in being known as the fixer, the helper, and the strategist on-demand.

I was heartbroken at how many years I'd spent giving of myself—my presence, my intellect, my wisdom and guidance—to people who weren't deserving. No matter how many tears I cried, nothing seemed to lessen the hurt.

And I had no idea what to do about any of it.

Although the word "healing" has become highly commodified in recent years, the work itself cannot be contained to beautifully packaged self-care purchases and social media posts. That is to say—you do not have to pay for the healing that our bodies are already trying to do naturally. Healing, in the context of personal transformation, is a process restoration. It involves acknowledging and accepting what we need to unlearn and let go, and confronting our pain with honesty and compassion in support of our well-being. Healing is about loving and nurturing ourselves—challenge by challenge, hurt by hurt, memory by memory—until we feel restored and in alignment with who we are, what we want, and how we live.

Assessing our Personal Wells is akin to going into a well that has been undisturbed for a long time. Whenever we are introspective, we start "troubling the waters" as the old folks like to say. All our stuff that has settled at the bottom is like sediment being brought to the surface. The water gets cloudy, murky, and discomfortingly dirty. That is the same thing that happens when we get clear on why we are so inclined to having and doing the most—our feelings rise and start swirling around in our heads and sitting heavy on our hearts. And just as we intuitively know when we need to care for ourselves by eating a good meal or getting adequate rest, we are equally aware when we need to heal. But far too often, we don't make or take time to do so.

There are many reasons why people avoid the healing process:

Sometimes, we believe the damage is done, and that nothing can fix the past.
Sometimes, we are too stuck on survival mode.
Sometimes, we confuse healing with weakness or failure.
Sometimes, we simply don't know where or how to begin.

And sometimes, most times, we are simply afraid of what we might uncover and how it will make us feel.

As you learn to heal your Personal Wells, you'll realize just how big a role our feelings play in our limiting beliefs and the choices we make. Because we simply don't like to feel difficult and uncomfortable feelings. So, instead of submitting ourselves to the process, we suppress, repress, or try to escape our emotions before we experience them.

Healing your Wells will require you to spend a lot of time with your Emotional and Historical Wells. Get *in* there! Go deep! And when your feelings inevitably start to rise, I want you to sit with the discomfort and allow yourself to feel them.

Say what you are feeling out loud:

I feel hurt and sad.
I feel used, abused, and betrayed.
I feel angry and upset.
I feel like I've wasted precious time and energy on people who could not care less about me.

Instead of trying to ignore how you really feel about what you've learned about yourself, take back your power by acknowledging and surrendering to your emotions.

Because what you have sacrificed in the past *has* cost you, and many of the investments you have made pouring into things, people, and businesses are sunk costs. But unless time travel becomes a reality, there's no way to go back and do things differently. You must allow yourself to feel the pain of that truth. And what you'll come to discover is something pretty astonishing: We tend to struggle with feeling the same three emotions: guilt, shame, and regret.

THE TRIFECTA TRAP: GUILT, SHAME, AND REGRET

Although humans can feel a range of emotions, we have our favorites, those feelings like love, happiness, and joy because they make us feel good inside. We are even open to allowing ourselves to feel a bit of anger here, and a bit of sadness there. And then, there are those feelings we avoid like the plague: guilt, shame, and regret. We'll do just about anything *not* to feel them! Which is how they become so easily rooted in our limiting beliefs.

Guilt

Few feelings are such a heavy weight to carry. Guilt creeps in whenever we feel that we have done something wrong or fallen short of who we believe we should be. Whether what we're feeling is because of a real wrongdoing or something we've imagined, guilt has a way of settling deep into our spirit and making us feel awful. It can cause us to become stressed, anxious, and even depressed.

At its core, guilt is often a reminder of the standards we hold for ourselves, which is why we must allow ourselves to feel the guilt, if for nothing else than to remind us that we aren't harming others when we choose to honor ourselves.

Shame

Much like guilt, few feelings cut as deeply as shame. When we feel ashamed, we don't just question what we've done—we start to question *who we are*. Shame tries to convince us that we are broken, unworthy, unlovable.

If guilt is trying to convince us, *I did something wrong*, our shame says something even more painful: *I am something wrong.*

Shame makes us want to hide, to shrink, to believe we are beyond repair. None of this is true. But, of course, we know this only once we allow ourselves to feel and experience what shame has come to show and teach us.

Even though shame can be a tough teacher, its lessons are invaluable. Shame shows us where we need to extend ourselves compassion. Because none of us is perfect. We are all works in progress. And when we choose to face shame instead of run from it, we give ourselves the chance to grow into who we're becoming—not who shame tries to convince us we'll always be.

Regret

Unlike feelings of guilt and shame, regret isn't about what we did wrong—it's about the choices we didn't make and the chances we didn't take. Regret has a way of lingering, quietly reminding us of what could have been.

Where guilt focuses on our actions and shame on Self, regret centers on the consequences we wish we could change. The missed opportunities. The words left unsaid. The doors we didn't walk through.

But regret, like all hard emotions, can also be one of life's teachers. How can it help us see where we long for more? What can it help us learn about how to choose differently if there's a next time? If we let it, regret can be a compass that guides us away from the lives we are seeking freedom from and toward a future we still have time to create.

If we are not careful, guilt, shame, and regret can easily become the trifecta trap, keeping us tethered to the expectations of others, and convincing us that disappointing someone else is the worst thing we can do. But the truth is, we have to face our feelings regardless. And what we ultimately learn is that, like all feelings, guilt, shame, and regret are fleeting. We allow ourselves to feel them . . . and move on. Allowing ourselves to feel is how we heal our Personal Wells.

Likewise, we have to be prepared to experience loss when we make the brave decision to start choosing ourselves. When we let go of the limiting beliefs, when we shed the identities that no longer serve us, when we allow ourselves to experience the feelings that come with disappointing others, we discover what connections in our life are transactional versus those that are genuine. It is another aspect of personal liberation that you will have to learn to accept and heal from: Loss is the cost of living in alignment.

THE NECESSITY OF LOSS

It should come as no surprise that choosing ourselves often results in losing others. While this is especially true for transactional relationships, it can also happen with any interpersonal relationship, including blood relatives and friends we consider our chosen family. And these losses can be devastating.

For people pleasers and those whose love language is acts of service, the severing of relationships in which we invested so much of ourselves can also feel demoralizing. Whether this occurs in the workplace or within our interpersonal circles, we are forced to reckon with uncomfortable truths. We must acknowledge the need to sever what we believed to be unbreakable bonds. We must forgive ourselves for what we failed to see (or chose to ignore) in the relationship dynamic. We must let go—allowing ourselves to fully process the unavoidable, undeniable, unthinkable loss. We must try our best to move forward, to move on, sometimes with the pain of knowing there is nothing left to salvage.

I'll be honest, I naively believed that my previous work of letting go of things that no longer served me would have somewhat prepared me for the loss I'd experience. But I was completely unprepared for how I would feel when people let *me* go because I no longer served *them*. Ultimately, I would learn that loss is necessary. If we want to be free, if we want to be well, we cannot remain tethered to unhealthy relationships.

As someone who spent all her childhood and much of her adulthood focused on pleasing and helping others, by the time I was forty years old I had a vast network of people I considered friends. That *I* considered friends—I think that it is of the upmost importance to make that distinction. Because if we want to heal, we must acknowledge our own culpability for the role we played in our overwhelm. And the truth is, I created relationship dynamics that were rooted more in what I could do for others than in genuine connection.

Not that I came to this realization on my own, of course. This is actually a truth I was told by my Reiki practitioner, Sam Pendleton. During a session, I'd shared how overwhelmed I was because people were always asking me for something. I expressed being overwhelmed *and* annoyed, to be exact.

> "You're upset because whatever you were needing to be needed in that way . . . you no longer need to be needed in that way. But as you release these relationships, it is your responsibility to be gentle. Because you created these monsters."
> —Samantha "Sam" Pendleton, Reiki practitioner/SEED

Whew!

That is what happens when we find ourselves up against the trifecta trap. If we do not allow ourselves to surrender to how we feel when we say no, not only do we end up doing the most to the point of overwhelm, we also end up creating monsters who expect and demand the most from us. And when we are afraid to disappoint the monsters we've created, we can easily find ourselves once again overwhelmed.

A LOVE NOTE TO BLACK WOMEN

Loss Is Inevitable

Of all the narratives within the ever-growing body of scholarly research on the transatlantic slave trade and American slavery, I have an affinity for stories of rebellion and resistance. From the sands of the Gold Coast to the Middle Passage, there is substantial evidence that many Africans who were stolen and sold for exploitation and labor did not go willingly. They stormed the decks of ships to overtake captains and crews. They killed their captors with poison they made themselves. They even jumped into the ocean, succumbing to death on their own terms rather than continuing on their treacherous journey.

In the Deep South, researchers and historians have archived thousands of "wanted" posters for fugitive slaves. A select few bore a headline that initially baffled those studying the era: "runaway by design." Later, it was discovered this was a designation for a special class of fugitive slaves, a warning of sorts. Because despite the number of times they had been captured and returned to their owners, "runaways by design" *kept* running away! Their spirits so determined, their hearts and minds so steadfast, they'd never stop chasing liberation until they found it.

From the post-antebellum South to the Great Migration to the civil rights era and our present-day fight for equal rights and liberties, the history of Black Americans is rife with stories of seeking freedom. But the narratives of enslaved people escaping the horrors of Southern plantations are in a class all their own, which is why they serve as an anchor for this book.

Nothing that you are facing on your journey to liberation can even remotely compare to what folks encountered and endured in the past. You *can* and *will* get free from an unwell life filled with overwhelm. And, more importantly, you can and will *stay* free.

Although not every effort to escape the confines of enslavement was successful, each documented story of self-emancipation provides invaluable insight, particularly regarding the mindset one had to have to even *attempt* to seek freedom under such treacherous conditions. Regardless of the outcome, one common thread exists. Anyone seeking freedom had no choice but to leave someone or something behind: Elders they'd been taught to honor. Infants and children they'd birthed and loved. Favorite items too bulky to carry. Keepsakes that, the longer they remained untouched, might buy more time to cover more distance. Not to mention a familiarity, regardless of how horrific, versus an unknown fate.

To even *attempt* to seek freedom, one had to be willing to accept loss.

Some losses are necessary. Sometimes leaving behind what no longer serves us is the only way to ensure we can be well.

Embracing loss is about making peace with what was, honoring what your experiences taught you, and trusting that who and what remains is enough. It is learning to release what no longer serves you with gratitude, even when it hurts. Experiencing loss is not something we can escape. Often, loss is something we carry for a lifetime—we learn to live with the memories of what no longer remains. The only way to move forward is to give ourselves permission to grieve what we have let go in order to find freedom from our lives of overwhelm.

THE NECESSITY OF GRIEF

Grief is a natural and inevitable response to loss, whether it involves the loss of a loved one, a relationship, a dream, or even a sense of self. It is often viewed with resistance, discomfort, and a desire to bypass it as quickly as possible. However, what many fail to realize is that grief is not just something to get through—it's a process that, if fully experienced, carries with it the unexpected and beautiful gift of healing. Healing is the bonus gift that emerges when we allow ourselves to go through the full journey of grieving, embracing its pain and its lessons along the way.

At its core, grieving is an emotional and psychological response that is both deeply personal and profoundly transformative. The early stages of grief are marked by feelings of shock, disbelief, anger, and profound sadness. These feelings can be overwhelming, and the instinct to avoid or suppress them is strong. Yet, when we allow ourselves to experience these emotions rather than avoid them, we create an opportunity for healing. The pain of grief is, paradoxically, a doorway to restoration. It is through confronting and expressing the emotions tied to our loss that we begin to heal. Ignoring or repressing grief can lead to prolonged emotional distress, as the unresolved feelings linger, often manifesting as physical symptoms, anxiety, or depression.

Grief forces us to reckon with the reality of change. Change is difficult, and the loss of something or someone important forces us to adapt to a new way of being. While this can initially feel like a disorienting and painful experience, it is also a chance for growth. As we go through the process of grieving, we slowly find new ways of understanding our lives and our identities. We gain insights about ourselves, our capacity for love, and our resilience. Over time, we begin to reframe our experience of loss—not as something that simply takes away from us, but as something that reshapes us, often in ways we couldn't have imagined before.

The act of grieving allows us to reestablish a connection with the person, thing, or idea we have lost. This doesn't mean that we move on as if nothing ever happened, but rather that we learn how to carry the memory or the essence of what we've lost with us in a way that does not diminish us. It becomes a part of our new reality, and we begin to heal by integrating that loss into our ongoing narrative. Through this process, we may discover a newfound strength or a sense of peace we never expected.

Ultimately, grieving is not just about letting go—it is about growing through the loss. The process might be uncomfortable, but by embracing it, we gain a deeper understanding of life's fragility and our own strength. Healing comes not from avoiding the pain of grief, but from allowing ourselves to journey through it with openness, honesty, and self-compassion. The bonus gift of healing is found not in the absence of pain, but in the wisdom, growth, and peace that come from experiencing the full emotional range of grief. It is, indeed, a process worth undergoing, for on the other side lies the gift of restoration and a renewed sense of Self.

Grief is an act of surrender. And it is truly a gift.

For many years, I believed that grieving—the act of mourning loss—was reserved for personal tragedies or the loss of a loved one. Grieving was for sicknesses and accidents where death seemed imminent. Or for the wakes and funerals of those who recently died. Sure, I'd heard many idioms about grief. I even wrongly quoted and attributed some, such as an elephant never forgets, unaware that this fact is tied to their grief: For years, elephants return to the places where members of their herd have died to cradle their bones in their tusks.

Much like elephants, we too rarely forget who and what we've lost. The only difference is rarely do we acknowledge and grieve the pain. But we must.

Grieving is integral to our personal liberation.

You must grieve your past. The person you once were. The mistakes you made and the lessons you learned. The you who loved people who weren't deserving. The you who believed lies and accepted less than what you deserved. The people-pleasing, self-sacrificing, self-sabotaging you. The you that you hate to think about because you loathe that version of yourself.

You must grieve the time you can't get back. The love that may never be reciprocated. The money spent, the resources wasted. The people you allowed to use and abuse you because you were too afraid to leave and be alone.

You must grieve your decisions. What you didn't say and didn't do. What you might have accomplished or achieved. Where you might have moved or traveled to. Who you should have clung to harder, who you should have let go sooner. How much you didn't know, how much you should have known.

Sometimes, you must simply grieve life itself. Not just the past, but to even allow yourself to feel anticipatory grief. Because to live is to also know that nothing, absolutely nothing, lasts forever.

Grieving itself is an act of liberation.

GRIEF: THE LOVE IN LOSS

The language and psychology regarding the complexities of parenting and how our childhood heavily influences our adult relationships has changed significantly over the years. What are now commonly known as mother and father wounds once went by a different term: abandonment.

For much of my life, I held many limiting beliefs about what it meant to be an abandoned daughter. And for much of my life, it was a label I allowed to define who I was and how I loved. Years of therapy helped me identify my triggers, my struggle with trust, and the behaviors that activated my anxiety in relationships. But what helped me *heal* was grieving my father—earthside during his final days in hospice and in the spiritual realm after he died.

The day I received the call that my father was in the hospital, I remember it feeling surreal. As a little girl, I had memories of getting dressed on Saturday morning and spending the day staring out the window, watching and waiting for him to arrive. Disappointment after disappointment, so much so that I carried the limiting belief that all men would disappoint me well into adulthood.

As a young woman, I was angry at him. So angry that I remember saying, “I cannot wait until he’s on his deathbed. I cannot wait to abandon him just like he abandoned me.”

But I was much older, in my early forties, when I got the call.

I hung up the phone and cried, surprised by my reaction upon hearing that cancer was quickly destroying the body of a man I barely knew. Surprised that receiving “the” phone call did not bring the joy I once thought it would.

My father is dying.

I recall arriving at hospice. How the staff had come to meet me because it seemed the only words my father had to say for the past two days were, “My daughter is coming!”

“Before we take you back, can you please answer a few questions, verify a few things for me?” one of the hospice nurses asked.

“Sure, I can try,” I’d offered. But when I saw her pull out the paperwork, I knew I’d be little to no help at all.

"Can you confirm his address?"

"No."

"Can you confirm his date of birth?"

"No."

"Can you confirm his social security number?"

"No."

She looked dumbfounded, confused that the daughter my father had bragged about coming knew nothing about him.

"I'm sorry," I said quietly. "This is only the third time I'm seeing him in my life."

We walked to his room in silence. Before the nurse left, she turned to me and smiled. "God bless you."

I realized that, for me, I'd spoken a truth I rarely shared with others. For her, it was highly unlikely that I was the first person to visit a parent they barely knew.

My father's eyes brightened when he saw me. And then just as quickly he looked away. But it was too late—I'd already seen his feelings pooling in his eyes. Guilt, shame, and regret. Joy, happiness, closure, and peace.

My dad.

We talked for a bit before he fell asleep, nodding off as he held my hand. I sat there for a while, grateful to know I'd have time for a few more visits before he became an ancestor. I took a picture of my hand in his, and when I got back to the hotel, I cried. I grieved as I wrote these words:

> 5/30/19—This is my father's hand. It's so odd to write those five words because I'm holding the hand of a stranger. It's odd to be here, in hospice, concerned for his well-being, pain levels, and comfort. It's odd to have compassion, and even more surprisingly, to be experiencing a range of emotions for someone I do not know. My parents divorced when I was two years old. The last childhood memory I have of my father is from grade school—going to his house to get five dollars for a new lunchbox. Then, over thirty years

> later, I had lunch with him—wanting an apology, hopeful for a new beginning, and if not, at least closure. I received neither. And now, almost a decade later, here we are. The past twenty-four hours have been a blur of signing consents, making travel arrangements, and having a long-overdue conversation with my daughter. It's all . . . something. I never thought I'd be here. (Spending his years with regret and remorse was supposed to be his punishment.) But, forgiveness. Everything is odd and strange and surreal, but I'm here. And it's more sweet than bitter. It's the last remnants of a healing that I didn't know I needed. Speaking to the staff and seeing their smiles. "We're glad you're here. He's been asking, 'When is my daughter arriving? She said she's coming!'" Waiting for Nalah to get out of school so she can FaceTime us because she "has to meet him." So many moments of generational healing—of disclosing secrets and disappointment, of forgiveness and love. Sharing this because I know my story is not unique. And because what I know having been married and divorced is that marriage and divorce are hard. What I know as a mother is that parenting is hard. What I know is that most people try—whatever that means for them—and often it falls nowhere close to the expectations we have for them. And so. I'm here. In hospice. Holding the hand of my eighty-year-old father for the first time. I am here in this odd, sweet, sad space. And I'm thankful. Taking it moment by moment.

And I would grieve him—the father I didn't get to have until the day he died and years after. The father who, on his deathbed, told me he loved me for the first and only time in my life.

Grief, I realized, is the love forever embedded in loss.

My father's death taught me that grief is not something to be feared, avoided, or silenced. Rather, grief is an invitation to honor ourselves by acknowledging what we've lost. To name what is no longer a part of our lives. And to experience the spectrum of emotions that grief often brings—sadness, anger, confusion, and sometimes surprisingly, even regret.

Loss and grief are simply the rhythm of healing—the ebb and flow of release and renewal. So trust that every moment is guiding you toward the liberating life you want and deserve. A life that is worth protecting everything you healed from and for.

CHAPTER 6

PROTECT THE WELLS

Protecting our Personal Wells isn't something that we can leave to chance. It is something we must decide and be intentional about following through on. And that decision often begins with being selfish in the ways that matter most. Not selfish in the distorted sense we've been taught to fear, but selfish in the way that honors your time, your energy, your relationships, your resources, and your sanity.

Because once we've done the work of being introspective, of letting go, of grieving and healing, we have to protect ourselves. We have to guard our Personal Wells from the patterns and expectations that once drained us. Otherwise, we risk slipping back into the cycles of depletion that caused us to seek liberation in the first place.

This is where we start establishing the terms of our liberation. This is where we say:

I am no longer available for what drains me.
I am no longer willing to sacrifice my well-being to meet someone else's expectations.

It's about making choices that serve the life we're building, not the life we've outgrown. And that means setting boundaries.

Saying no. Choosing less. And refusing to overextend ourselves for others' approval or validation.

Protecting our Wells means being clear about honoring our wellness and overall well-being.

Personal liberation is not only about releasing what no longer serves us. It's also about protecting what does. True freedom is creating space for the life we want to live and holding that space sacred.

THE NECESSITY OF SELFISHNESS

Selfishness has a bad reputation that it can't seem to shake. That is because we have been taught that being selfish means we're greedy, uncaring, or self-centered. I mean, just consider the dictionary's leading definition of the word:

> ***selfish***[1]
>
> *adj.* (of a person, action, or motive) lacking consideration for others

Yikes!

Unfortunately, this is the definition that most of us are familiar with—one that evokes an image of a horrible person who lacks sympathy and empathy for anyone other than themselves. And who wants to be thought of as someone who's like *that*?

But what if I told you there is another meaning noted in the dictionary? One that illustrates how being selfish is aligned with our goals for personal liberation?

selfish[2]

adj. concerned chiefly with one's own personal profit or pleasure

Umm, yes please!

It's the being "chiefly concerned" for me.

Discovering this definition was a game-changer for me. It removed the negative connotations that are commonly associated with selfishness, replacing them with a framework for how to prioritize oneself. Soon, I found myself saying, "Let me be chiefly concerned with myself," whenever I felt the urge to "help" or "intervene" when listening to others.

Being chiefly concerned for myself has lessened my overwhelm *significantly.*

When we strip away the stigma, "selfishness" is simply another word for survival. For honoring our boundaries. For choosing ourselves. For breaking free from the endless cycles of overwhelm and exhaustion of putting others' needs before our own. When it comes to our personal liberation, being selfish isn't something to feel guilty about—it's something we practice if we want to stay free.

Many of us were taught—by family, culture, and society—that putting ourselves first is wrong. And we were led to believe that our worth comes from how much we give, how much we endure, how well we serve the needs of others. We may have been praised for our selflessness even as it caused our overwhelm.

And we already know the consequences of living a life of constant self-sacrifice.

When we keep putting everyone else first, we drain our energy, our time, and our resources. We end up burned-out, resentful, disconnected from what we need and who we are. The belief that being selfish is wrong keeps us trapped—giving and giving until there's nothing left, which is why selfishness isn't a flaw.

It is a necessary, radical act of self-preservation.

SELFISHNESS, RESILIENCE, AND SELF-CARE

One of the most popular and profitable subsectors of the wellness industry is that of self-care. At its core, self-care is the practice of prioritizing the care and keeping of ourselves—our bodies, minds, hearts, and homes, which sounds an awful lot like . . . being chiefly concerned with our own personal profit and pleasure. Yet we rarely see selfishness associated with our wellness . . . which is ironic since we need to fully embrace being unapologetically selfish to commit to the act of self-care.

So why don't the good people of the wellness and self-care communities just say that?

Despite what we've been taught throughout our lives, there is nothing wrong with being selfish. We are, in fact, biologically wired to put our own needs and desires before others'. Our survival literally depends on it! But given the negative connotation, we tend to do whatever it takes to avoid being associated with being selfish, which, unfortunately, causes us to be less self-serving and more self-sacrificing. And the more we do of the latter, the more we contribute to our lives of overwhelm.

Not wanting to be seen as selfish is the reason we tend to say yes when we really want to say no. The reason we loan money we can't really afford to not be paid back and offer our expertise even though we do not really have the time or energy to give. The reason we stay in relationships and careers that have long since run their course. Fear of being seen or labeled as someone who lacks care and consideration for others keeps us bound to unfulfilling experiences and unrequited situations.

Which is why our liberation requires us to instead be honest and choose ourselves.

As with most life lessons, children can serve as examples of how to personify simple concepts we adults tend to make complex. Because selfishness is essentially making sure that your well-being is the priority. Yes, over everyone and everything else whenever feasible and as often as possible.

And no one exemplifies the art of being the priority like a child.

From birth and throughout early childhood, young people are unapologetic in their selfishness. When in infancy, babies cry whenever they are hungry or in need of nurturing. Toddlers prioritize their ever-changing demands in real time, regardless of their caregivers' efforts or feelings. "I know I said I wanted a peanut butter and jelly sandwich, but now I want eggs." If we are not laughing at their antics, we're on our knees praying we survive their sense of entitlement. Their behavior continues until they are old enough to understand and heed the words of an authority figure to "not be selfish" or suffer the consequences.

But we can learn a lot from watching children learn to navigate and balance the natural instinct to prioritize themselves over others' demands and expectations of them. These experiences clearly demonstrate how to exercise selfishness for one's own personal profit and pleasure.

This came to light early on in my journey, when I realized there was a trait that I took great pride in as a Black woman, one that I wore as a badge of honor: I was resilient. And I couldn't help but wonder what other signs and symptoms I'd missed over the years trudging through in the name of resiliency.

resilience[3]

noun. the capacity to withstand or to recover quickly from difficulties; toughness

"Resilience" was a word I specifically attributed to Black and brown folks who persevered despite the systems designed to disenfranchise us. I thought of resiliency as a gift, a blood memory passed down generationally from my ancestors. Not that those things weren't true. But I could not shake the feeling that there was more. So, with nothing but time on my hands, I did a deep dive into the meaning of resiliency.

To say that what I discovered was surprising would be an understatement.

In the medical field, resiliency is defined as the capacity to maintain or regain one's mental health despite experiencing challenging circumstances.[4] I recall how I felt as I read this definition over and over, becoming more and more unnerved and upset as I began to understand the full, complex meaning of the word. I'd never associated resiliency with my mental health. I thought it was something I "tapped into" whenever I needed to keep going instead of giving up. I'd also never considered resiliency from the perspective of capacity. I thought resiliency was an ancestor-gifted abundant resource running through my veins, the source of what made it possible for me to get through and get by no matter how the odds were stacked against me.

Could one of the traits I loved most about myself and my people also be one of the culprits contributing to the state of my physical, mental, and spiritual well-being?

It was a rhetorical question. Because I knew the answer: yes.

Although a useful quality that had undoubtedly helped me, my loved ones, and our ancestors survive, resiliency was not without its limits. Nor was it a state of being I was meant to embody at all times. I realized I'd spent much of my life in a constant state of trying to maintain or regain my sanity.

No wonder I was unwell!

A LOVE NOTE TO BLACK WOMEN

Resilience Has Its Limits

If there is one thing people of the African diaspora hold close to our hearts, it is the resilience woven into our lineage. Our legacy is steeped in survival, in endurance, in pushing through against all odds. And this is especially true for Black women. We are taught to be strong. To carry the weight of our families, our communities, our dreams—often without complaint, often at great cost to ourselves.

So, if you are feeling overwhelmed—if your body feels heavy, your spirit stretched thin—I want you to know that you are not alone. Chances are, you've been here before. Chances are, your body tried to tell you long before the overwhelm set in. Maybe there were quiet signs—a tension in your shoulders, an ache in your back, a lingering fatigue that rest never seemed to touch. Maybe you brushed them off, self-diagnosed, or told yourself it wasn't that bad. Maybe you had a gut feeling that something wasn't right—but you kept going. You kept pushing through. Because that's what we've been taught to do. To be resilient. To succeed. To chase the dream, no matter the cost.

And I get it. Not just in theory, but in practice. I know what it means to push past your own limits because the world told you that rest was a luxury you couldn't afford. I know how easily overwhelm becomes the baseline, how quickly unwell becomes normal. But

hear me when I say it: You deserve more. You deserve to be well. You deserve to feel whole. Your worth is not measured by how much you endure. Knowing and embodying this is a necessity on your journey of learning to honor yourself and your longing to be free.

One of the greatest benefits of embracing selfishness is the freedom it provides. Choosing to do less requires us to be selfish. It forces us to acknowledge that our time and energy are finite and that we cannot afford to waste them on things that do not serve us. When we learn to say no without guilt, we reclaim our power. When we prioritize our well-being, we become more present and engaged in the things that truly matter. When we stop seeking external validation and embrace our own needs, we find a sense of inner peace that no amount of people-pleasing can provide.

So, once we decide to be chiefly concerned with ourselves, what can we do to make sure we practice selfishness as an act of self-love, self-preservation, and self-care? We can establish our TERMS for liberation to ensure we prioritize our wellness and overall well-being.

THE NECESSITY OF TERMS

As it was for many Black teens and young adults, hip-hop was my first introduction into activism and a form of political protest so different from that of the civil rights era of my parents' generation. To me, it seemed the perfect form of creative expression: poetic lyrics over tight beats that made it impossible not to remember the message promoting social change.

I had quite the collection of politically charged hip-hop albums thanks to Columbia House's music club (oh, what a time to be alive), including Dead Prez's debut album, *Let's Get Free.* So imagine my surprise nearly twenty years later when I found myself in Lululemon's Community Coalition with none other than Stic himself.

Although he was now far removed from Dead Prez musical performances, there was something special about discovering that Stic was still a social activist and now also an author and vegetarian. Of course, he still had his suave way about him. And he was, of course, still incredibly brilliant.

Everyone in the Community Coalition gravitated toward his quiet style of speaking only when necessary, especially because whenever he did speak, we knew he'd be sharing something profound. Every session, every single session, we'd wait patiently for Stic to bless us with some divine guidance. Sometimes, we'd get a few sentences. Other times, a short monologue. Regardless, every time, every single time, Stic's wisdom was exactly what we needed. All the support offered by the teachers and coaches that attended and facilitated our meetings was so needed.

We'd all been selected to join the Community Coalition for the leadership roles we held within our respective communities. And we were all profoundly overwhelmed by doing our already difficult work during a new, unprecedented time. Our weekly meetings were held over Zoom and included a mixture of exercise, instructive guidance, and lessons on how to prioritize caring for ourselves. The biggest lesson for me happened the day our session focused on the power of saying no, which also happened to be the session where Stic changed my life.

One of the fearless leaders spearheading the Community Coalition was Robbie Tubajon, now vice president of performance and leadership development at Pro Athlete Community. Robbie was our everything—our personal trainer, our life coach, our mentor, our cheerleader, and a much-needed comedian with an infectious smile. When he smiled in a particular way, his eyes lighting up at the opportunity to change our lives through a difficult exercise or lifestyle challenge, I knew the day's session was going to kick my ass. In a good way. But usually in a way I was totally unprepared for.

"Who wants to be in the hot seat today?" Robbie asked, his smile letting us know that what he really meant was "Who wants to volunteer as tribute?"

Being in the hot seat meant not only were you participating in the session's lesson but also that *you* were the lesson. Being in the hot seat meant you would be an integral part of a teachable moment. Because that was the purpose: to bring about personal transformative change, which often moved the entire Community Coalition to transformative tears.

"Who needs to learn how to say no?" Robbie's eyes darted across the screen as he glanced at each member of the Coalition. In my heart of hearts, I knew the topic of this session was looking and waiting for me.

Despite being in leadership roles for more than a decade, "no" was a word I'd still not learned to wield as the powerful weapon it is. Not that I didn't want to say no. On the contrary, I wanted to say it all the time. But I just . . . I couldn't. The people pleaser in me simply could not bring herself to disappoint others by declining their asks and offers.

"Me," I said, raising my hand high in the air. "Me. I need to learn how to say no. Desperately."

Just as I imagined, it was a tough session. I had truly volunteered as tribute. Robbie and the life coach leading the session were kind, of course, but honest, brutally honest. And each question I had to answer forced me to dig deeper into the source of my people-pleasing. It should come as no surprise that when we finally got to the root of it, my struggles with saying no started in childhood with the unrealistic expectation that I needed to be a good girl all the time.

It was a difficult acknowledgment, a painful revisiting of a moment in childhood that forever altered my life from being my older brother's little sister to becoming the responsible daughter. A weighted burden I'd carried into adulthood that had ultimately become a major contributor to my life of overwhelm.

Although the session was grueling, it was wonderful to have the support of fellow cohort members. All of us were leaders in our community in our respective capacities, which meant everyone understood the challenges I faced being bombarded with meaningful requests. It is one thing to decline a meetup for coffee with a stranger who wants to "pick your brain" for free advice. It is something altogether different when the request is from a teacher at a Title I school whose students want to meet the author of the first books where they saw themselves on the page.

"Sometimes you just have to say no," the facilitator encouraged gently. "It is not being mean. It is not being a bad person. It is being honest about your capacity."

"But it's so hard," I shared. "Some of the asks I receive are hard to decline because of the impact. Like, knowing that if I say yes it could change someone's life makes it harder to say no."

Listen, I meant that sincerely. But let me assure you—you alone are not the only person who can change someone's life. That is an enormous amount of pressure to put on yourself and also, it is simply not true. But it was definitely a limiting belief I had at the time. If I say no, what's going to happen? Spoiler: They'll find someone else.

"You know what, Christine? You just need to establish your terms. And before you say yes to anything, ask yourself: Is this on my terms?"

It was Stic, which meant all of us, even the facilitator, prepared to capture the wisdom we were about to receive. Life-changing wisdom that, with Stic's blessing, I am now sharing with you.

TERMS FOR LIBERATION

Before you say yes, ask yourself: Is this request on my TERMS?

The T stands for *time*. Before you say yes, ask yourself: Do I truly have the time and availability to do this?

The E stands for *energy*. If you do have the time, before you say yes, ask yourself: Do I have the energy to do this? Or, if the ask isn't immediate, will I have the energy to do this?

The R stands for *relationships*. If you have the time and energy, before you say yes, ask yourself: Is this a relationship that is meaningful? A relationship that I want to establish or continue nurturing? Or is it a one-off request that is only going to benefit the other party?

The M stands for *money*. If you have the time and the energy, and this is a relationship you value, ask yourself: Are they paying you what you want and what you're worth? And if there isn't a monetary benefit, is the work worth it to you for other reasons?

The S stands for *sanity*. Even if you have the time and the energy, this is a relationship you value, and they are willing to pay you what you're worth, ask yourself: Will this cost me my sanity? Because nothing and no one is worth your sanity.

If the answer to any of the above is no, the ask is simply not on your TERMS and you should decline.

I still laugh whenever I think about him suggesting that I put TERMS on a sticky note above my desk, on my computer, or wherever I needed to, so I'd see it whenever I got a request. Sticky note? I was strongly considering getting TERMS tattooed on my wrist!

Since then, it remains the framework I use to ensure I am selfish about my most valuable resources: my time, my energy, my relationships, my money, and most importantly, my sanity. More than anything, it taught me to pause. To take a moment to really think about what is being asked, who is asking, and what would truly be required of me.

TERMS is a great framework to help us decipher *when* to say no. But of course, we actually have to say it, which, if we do not know *how* to speak our truth, can leave us feeling immobilized. Given our overwhelming past, we know that saying no, especially in the moment, can be challenging. Especially for those of us who have never experienced boundaries modeled in a healthy dynamic—platonic, romantic, familial, or otherwise. And it is important to note that does not always mean the dynamic was toxic or abusive.

As someone who grew up without seeing conflict resolution, one of the limiting beliefs that contributed to my people-pleasing was that I genuinely believed saying yes and being self-sacrificing was akin to showing others how much I loved them or valued our connection. "No" was reserved for people I did not know or like enough to be in service to. And you already know how *that* worked out for me.

The truth is, regardless of how confident or self-assured someone appears outwardly, it does not necessarily correlate with how they feel inwardly when faced with the need to say no. In a recent study by the Thriving Center of Psychology, a thousand Americans were polled to better understand the challenges people face with setting healthy boundaries. The study found that 58 percent of Americans admit to having difficulty saying no, and that 65 percent of women admitted to struggling with saying no compared to 49 percent of men.

Additionally, researchers found this trend to be more pronounced among younger generations:

- 64 percent of Gen Zers
- 59 percent of millennials
- 55 percent of Gen Xers
- 42 percent of baby boomers

In a recent study published in the *Journal of Personality and Social Psychology*,[5] researchers found that 77 percent of people fear rejecting others due to concerns about potential negative consequences. All this to say: You are not alone.

But even more importantly, you are about to be empowered to no longer fear or feel guilty about saying no.

Because in order to live a liberated life, "no" is your superpower.

Of course, like any muscle that hasn't been used or is underdeveloped, initially you may struggle with setting boundaries. But I promise it gets easier. Because with each "no," you feel stronger and more unapologetically selfish.

THIRTY-ONE WAYS TO SAY NO

1. I can't commit to that right now, but I appreciate the offer.
2. I've got other priorities at the moment.
3. That's not something I can take on right now, thank you.
4. I need to pass this time, but I hope you understand.
5. I'm not able to, but I appreciate you thinking of me.
6. I'm going to have to decline, but thanks for asking.
7. That doesn't work for me, but I hope you find the right fit.
8. I'm focusing on something else right now, so I have to say no.
9. I respect that request, but I need to say no for now.
10. I have to honor my boundaries and say no this time.
11. That's not in alignment with my current priorities.
12. I'd love to help, but my plate is full.
13. I'm choosing to focus my energy elsewhere.
14. I'm not available for that, but I hope it works out for you.
15. I appreciate the invitation, but I won't be able to make it.
16. That's not something I'm able to do right now.
17. I don't have the capacity to take that on.
18. That doesn't fit into my schedule at the moment.
19. I won't be able to participate, but I'm cheering you on!

20. I'm prioritizing my well-being, so I'll have to decline.
21. That's not a commitment I can make right now.
22. I trust you'll find the right person for this, but it's not me.
23. I appreciate you asking, but I have to sit this one out.
24. I won't be able to give this the attention it deserves, so I'll have to say no.
25. That's not something I can make time for.
26. I'm focusing on things that align with my goals, so I'll have to pass.
27. I'm unable to take this on, but I hope you find a great solution.
28. I need to be intentional with my time, so I have to say no.
29. I'm honored you thought of me, but I can't commit to that.
30. I need to protect my time and energy, so I won't be able to do that.
31. That's not a yes for me, but I appreciate you reaching out.

You know your TERMS, and saying no is how you stand on business.

PART III

THE LIFESTYLE

CHAPTER 7

FACETS OF FREEDOM

Liberation is a word we often associate with revolution, breaking chains, and a dramatic shedding of everyone and everything that once confined us. Sometimes, that is indeed what it feels to be liberated. Sometimes, there is more.

Personal freedom is beautifully layered. In addition to being an experience, it is also a mindset that we embody. Because living a liberated life requires us to do the same work that set us free: We must continue to make courageous choices to ensure we are chiefly concerned with our own profit and pleasure.

You have done what is necessary to escape the life you were seeking freedom from. You know how to self-assess your Personal Wells. You know that loss is not something to be afraid of because letting go is how we heal. You know how to protect yourself by standing on your TERMS. You are no longer in survival mode or longing to be free from overwhelm—you are free! And being intentional about your choices is how you stay free.

There have been many surprises on my journey to personal liberation, yet there is only one that I continue to experience daily: Even after doing everything I've done to get free, I am still susceptible to reverting to my people-pleasing default mode. If I am not mindful, I can still find myself following my inner voice's unhinged advice based on old limiting beliefs.

Please know that it takes time to unlearn everything we have been taught about our worth being defined by how much we achieve, how well we perform, and how little we inconvenience others. And this unlearning happens day by day, moment by moment, choice by choice. With each decision, we discover what is at the core of liberatory work—being brave enough to stay true to who you are and what you stand for regardless of others' approval.

HONORING OUR FREEDOM, HONORING OURSELVES

Living a liberated life requires the same mindset to live in alignment. It means you are fully committed to being true to yourself, your values, your needs, and your vision for the life you want and deserve. And we know we are in alignment because of how we feel when we make choices that are congruent with who we are and what matters most.

Alignment does not mean life is always easy or completely devoid of overwhelm. It simply means we are intentional about honoring ourselves with every decision and in every thing we do. Being liberated from others' validation and expectations is how we move through life with integrity, not out of obligation.

But staying *in* alignment isn't always simple. We are constantly evolving, and so are our circumstances. What once felt aligned may begin to feel tight or outgrown. That's why alignment requires regular check-ins—a willingness to pause and ask, Is this still true for me? Is this still mine? That's where the facets of freedom come in.

Each facet offers a lens—a gentle litmus test—for exploring how aligned you feel in that area of your life. When you're emotionally free, your feelings flow instead of fester. When you're mentally free, your beliefs support your growth instead of limit it. When you're spiritually free, your faith feels like a homecoming, not a performance. These facets are not goals to chase or boxes to check; they are mirrors and maps. They help you notice where your life feels expansive and where it feels constrained—where you're leading from intention, and where you might still be led by fear, habit, or expectation.

Coming into alignment isn't a one-time arrival—it's a lifelong practice. The more you learn to listen to yourself, the easier it becomes to recognize when something is off. And the more you honor those cues, the more your life begins to reflect your truth—not just in what it looks like, but in how it feels. These facets can guide you back to yourself again and again, each time with more grace, more clarity, and more freedom.

You don't need to master them all. You don't need to start at the beginning. You simply need to start. Your freedom doesn't have to be loud to be real. It just has to be yours.

Freedom doesn't live in just one area of our lives. It lives in the spaces where we feel safe to be honest. Where we feel empowered to choose differently. Where we are no longer bound by expectations that silence our truth or deny our joy. True wellness isn't compartmentalized—it's holistic. And so is liberation.

The facets of freedom offer a new way to explore what it means to live in alignment—with your values, your body, your energy, your purpose. Think of them as windows into different parts of your life, each one revealing where you feel most free and where you might still feel confined or overwhelmed. They are not rigid categories or boxes to check. They are invitations to pause, reflect, and return to yourself.

EMOTIONAL FREEDOM

Emotional freedom is the ability to feel and express our emotions fully—without guilt, fear, or suppression. It's a sacred space where we give ourselves permission to be honest about what we feel, even when those emotions are messy, inconvenient, or misunderstood. This facet of wellness requires vulnerability, self-compassion, and a commitment to choosing peace over performance. It's not about staying in our feelings forever but allowing them to move through us so we can heal and grow. True emotional freedom includes releasing resentment, making peace with our past, and honoring our present emotional landscape without shame.

Yet many of us are taught—explicitly or implicitly—that our emotions are something to hide or fix. We carry the limiting belief that if we express what we truly feel, we'll be seen as weak, dramatic, or "too much." This belief often stems from early life experiences where emotional expression was met with criticism, rejection, or silence. Over time, we begin to disconnect from our emotional Selves, suppressing what we feel to preserve relationships, reputations, or routines. We wear emotional masks that protect us from judgment, but they also keep us from authenticity and healing.

A more liberating belief is this: "Expressing my emotions is a courageous act of self-respect."

When we allow ourselves to feel and speak our truth, we begin to build deeper trust with ourselves and others. We stop apologizing for our sensitivity and start recognizing it as a strength. Emotional freedom doesn't mean broadcasting every feeling—it means no longer abandoning ourselves to make others comfortable. It means choosing peace not by avoiding conflict but by honoring what's real. And from that place of honesty, we create space for genuine connection, inner calm, and lasting transformation.

Journaling prompt: *What emotions have I been avoiding or suppressing lately, and what might they teach me if I allowed myself to feel them fully?*

MENTAL FREEDOM

Mental freedom is the clarity that comes when your mind is no longer clouded by "shoulds," outdated narratives, and inherited expectations. It's the liberation from limiting beliefs, societal conditioning, and thought patterns that keep you playing small or stuck in cycles of self-doubt.

This facet of wellness invites us to reclaim our mental space—to challenge the thoughts that confine us and to replace them with beliefs that support our growth, wholeness, and joy. Mental freedom doesn't mean having a silent or perfect mind; it means having an empowered relationship with your thoughts.

Still, many people live with the limiting belief that their thoughts are facts. If we think we're unworthy, behind, or not good enough, we assume it must be true. Add to that the weight of generational expectations, cultural norms, and societal pressures, and it becomes easy to internalize messages that were never ours to carry. We begin to shape our lives around "shoulds"—what we should want, how we should behave, who we should become. This mental noise can drown out our intuition and stifle our ability to think for ourselves.

A more liberating belief is: "Not every thought is true, and I have the power to choose which ones I follow."

Mental freedom begins when we pause to question the stories we've inherited and decide which ones are worth keeping. It's a practice of intentional thinking—of catching ourselves when we spiral into fear, comparison, or self-judgment and choosing a more loving, grounded thought instead. When we free our minds, we begin to hear ourselves more clearly. We remember who we are underneath the noise, and from that clarity, we can make aligned, authentic choices with confidence and grace.

Journaling prompt: *What beliefs or thought patterns do I keep repeating that no longer serve me? Whose voice do they really belong to—and what's a more loving truth I can replace them with?*

PHYSICAL FREEDOM

Physical freedom is the ability to move, rest, and exist in your body with ease and care. It's about honoring your body's natural rhythms and treating it not as a project to fix, but as a home to nurture. This facet of wellness invites us to reconnect with our physical Selves—to notice how we feel, what we need, and how we carry ourselves through the world. Physical freedom also includes releasing anything that physically weighs us down, from cluttered spaces to chronic stress, overstimulation, or exhaustion. It's the liberation that comes from living in alignment with what your body is truly asking for.

Many of us carry the limiting belief that our bodies are only valuable when they are productive, attractive, or performing. We push ourselves past the point of fatigue, ignore signs of burnout, and deprioritize rest in a culture that celebrates constant doing. Over time, our bodies become repositories for stress and tension, and our spaces often reflect that same overwhelm. The clutter in our homes, schedules, or environments becomes a reflection of what we've been carrying internally: unprocessed emotions, unmet needs, and the weight of saying yes when we meant no.

A more liberating belief is this: "My body is worthy of care, comfort, and compassion—just as it is."

Physical freedom begins when we stop punishing ourselves for needing rest or for existing outside of narrow ideals. It's about creating environments that support our well-being and letting go of the pressure to push through. When we treat our bodies as sacred, we naturally begin to declutter our homes and reevaluate our habits and hustle.

Journaling prompt: *What is my body asking for right now—more movement, more rest, more care, or more release? What can I let go of in my space or schedule to feel lighter in my body?*

FINANCIAL FREEDOM

Financial freedom is having enough resources to make decisions based on desire and alignment—not just survival or necessity. It's the ability to say yes to what nourishes you and no to what drains you without fear of financial instability. This facet of wellness is about more than wealth—it's about choice, security, and dignity. It's about feeling empowered when it comes to your money, trusting yourself to manage it well, and building a life where your finances support your values rather than dictate your limitations. Financial freedom invites us to step out of scarcity and into sovereignty.

Still, many of us are raised with the limiting belief that money is either a source of shame or struggle. We're taught to fear not having enough or to believe we must sacrifice our peace to earn more. These beliefs can lead us to overwork, under recharge, or stay in situations that are misaligned simply because they feel "safe." Financial decisions become rooted in survival rather than possibility. And for those who've experienced generational poverty or economic instability, the fear of not having enough can become deeply internalized and difficult to release.

A more liberating belief is this: "I deserve financial ease, and I can build a life where money flows in alignment with my values."

Financial freedom begins with trusting that your worth isn't tied to your bank account—and that your financial story can be rewritten. Whether it means setting boundaries around spending, asking for a salary that you're worth, or simply believing that abundance is available to you, reclaiming your financial power is an act of self-liberation. It's not about chasing excess—it's about choosing enough, knowing you're enough, and living with a sense of financial peace and possibility.

Journaling prompt: *When I think about money, what feelings come up—fear, guilt, pride, scarcity, peace? How would my life change if I truly believed I deserved financial ease and dignity?*

CREATIVE FREEDOM

Creative freedom is the space and permission to explore, express, and innovate without fear of judgment or failure. It's the ability to follow your inspiration—not trends or expectations—and to create from a place of curiosity, authenticity, and joy. This facet of wellness is about reconnecting with your innate creativity, whether through art, ideas, problem-solving, or play. It's less about producing for praise and more about honoring your unique voice, vision, and way of seeing the world. Creative freedom is a reminder that expression itself is an act of liberation.

Yet many people carry the limiting belief that creativity is only for the talented, trained, or chosen few. We're taught to second-guess our ideas, to silence our creative urges, or to compare our expressions to polished final products. Fear of failure, criticism, or imperfection can stifle our creativity before it ever has a chance to take shape. Over time, we internalize the message that our creativity must have a purpose or profit to be worthy—and in doing so, we lose touch with the freedom to simply explore and express for the sake of our own fulfillment.

A more liberating belief is this: "My creativity is valuable because it is mine. I don't need permission to express it."

Creative freedom begins when we stop waiting for validation and start giving ourselves the space to try, to play, and to make without pressure. Whether it's a journal entry, a meal, a conversation, or a vision board, every act of creation becomes a reclamation of voice and agency. When we free ourselves from the need to be perfect or performative, we return to creativity as a source of joy, healing, and possibility—and in that space, something truly original is always waiting to emerge.

Journaling prompt: *When was the last time I created something purely for myself, and without the pressures of being good, perfect, or productive? What stories have I been told (or told myself) about who gets to be creative and why?*

SPIRITUAL FREEDOM

Spiritual freedom is the liberation that comes from living in alignment with your truth—whatever that looks like. It's about stepping into a personal, evolving connection with the divine that feels authentic, empowering, and deeply rooted in love. This facet of wellness invites us to trust our inner wisdom, to ask hard questions, and to find meaning on our own terms. Spiritual freedom is not about adhering to doctrine or tradition out of obligation; it's about choosing practices, beliefs, and rituals that nourish your soul and expand your sense of purpose, peace, and belonging.

Many people carry the limiting belief that spirituality must follow a certain path to be valid or that questioning inherited beliefs is a sign of disobedience or disrespect. For those raised in rigid traditions, spiritual shame can become a barrier to connection—leaving them feeling disconnected from both organized religion and their own intuitive guidance. The fear of "getting it wrong" spiritually can cause people to either cling tightly to dogma or abandon their spiritual Selves altogether. This all-or-nothing mindset can prevent the kind of intimate, liberating connection that spirituality is meant to offer.

A more liberating belief is this: "My spiritual path is mine to define, and I trust what resonates with my soul."

Spiritual freedom begins when we stop outsourcing our connection to the divine and begin cultivating it from within. Whether it's through prayer, meditation, nature, silence, or creativity, the divine reveals itself in countless ways—and we get to choose the practices that help us feel most grounded and connected. When we release fear and shame, we make room for reverence, wonder, and trust. Spiritual freedom isn't about having all the answers—it's about having the courage to seek, to question, and to walk in truth.

Journaling prompt: *What beliefs, practices, or traditions still resonate with my soul—and which ones feel heavy, inherited, or out of alignment? What does a truly personal connection to the divine look like for me?*

SOCIAL FREEDOM

Social freedom is the ability to set boundaries, leave unhealthy dynamics, and cultivate relationships rooted in mutual respect and authenticity. It's the power to choose connection over obligation, honesty over harmony, and presence over performance. This facet of wellness invites us to reimagine how we show up in community—not as who we think we should be, but as who we truly are. Social freedom honors our need for belonging and our right to individuality, reminding us that the healthiest relationships are those where we don't have to shrink, hide, or hustle for acceptance.

Many people carry the limiting belief that in order to be loved or accepted, they must tolerate disrespect, overextend themselves, or abandon their own needs. We're taught to prioritize politeness over truth, to keep the peace at any cost, and to equate being liked with being worthy. Over time, this leads to resentment, burnout, and disconnection—not just from others, but from ourselves. The fear of being alone or misunderstood can keep us tethered to relationships and social patterns that quietly diminish our self-worth.

A more liberating belief is this: "I deserve relationships where I can be fully myself, and it's safe to walk away from what no longer honors me."

Social freedom begins with the courage to set boundaries, speak your truth, and trust that the right people will honor your light. It's about creating space for nourishing connections and releasing anything that feels performative or extractive. When we stop trying to fit in and start choosing relationships where we belong, we experience a deeper, truer form of connection—one grounded in reciprocity, freedom, and love.

Journaling prompt: *Where am I staying silent, small, or overextended in my relationships? What boundary, truth, or goodbye would help me feel more authentic and respected in my connections?*

TIME FREEDOM

Time freedom is the ability to own your time and how it's spent. It's about living in a way that reflects your true priorities, not the demands of hustle culture, urgency, or other people's agendas. This facet of wellness invites you to slow down, to move with intention, and to reclaim time as a sacred and nonrenewable resource. Time freedom means choosing presence over productivity and redefining success as a life that feels spacious, not just busy. It's a quiet but radical refusal to measure your worth by how much you do or how fast you move.

Many people carry the limiting belief that they must constantly be in motion to be valuable. We're conditioned to equate busyness with importance and rest with laziness, internalizing the idea that there's never enough time and that every moment must be optimized or monetized. This belief keeps us stuck in cycles of overcommitment, rushing, and burnout. Even moments of rest can feel guilt-ridden or unearned, leaving us disconnected from our natural rhythms and exhausted by a pace that was never ours to begin with.

A more liberating belief is this: "Time is mine to shape, and I am allowed to move through life at my own pace."

Time freedom begins when we release the need to prove our worth through constant doing. It's about aligning your schedule with your values, making room for what matters most, and trusting that rest, reflection, and slowness are all necessary parts of a fulfilled life. When you begin to treat your time like the precious resource it is, you stop living on autopilot and start designing a life that actually feels like your own.

Journaling prompt: *If I could design a day that truly reflects my values and desires, how would I spend my time? What small shift could I make this week to move closer to that vision?*

IDENTITY FREEDOM

Identity freedom is the space to evolve, redefine, and show up as your full, complex, and ever-changing self—without apology. It's the right to outgrow past versions of you, to shift your values, passions, or appearance, and to expand beyond what others expect or understand. This facet of wellness honors the truth that identity is not fixed; it's fluid, layered, and deeply personal. Identity freedom invites you to live in alignment with who you are today, without needing to explain, justify, or shrink yourself to make others comfortable.

Yet many of us carry the limiting belief that we must remain consistent to be seen as trustworthy, stable, or successful. We're often praised for being predictable and penalized for changing. Over time, we internalize the fear that evolving will lead to rejection or loss—especially from those who've only known one version of us. This fear can keep us tethered to outdated labels, roles, or expectations that no longer reflect our truth. The result? We feel stuck, fragmented, and disconnected from our most authentic Selves.

A more liberating belief is this: "I am allowed to grow, and every version of me deserves love and acceptance."

Identity freedom begins when we give ourselves permission to change—again and again. It's about embracing our multidimensionality, owning our contradictions, and releasing the pressure to be understood by everyone. When we allow ourselves to show up fully, we make room for deeper self-acceptance and more honest relationships. In that freedom, we discover the courage to be who we are becoming—without fear, without apology, and without limits.

Journaling prompt: *What parts of myself have I outgrown but still hold onto? Who am I becoming—and what do I need to release in order to fully step into that version of me?*

PURPOSE FREEDOM

Purpose freedom is the ability to live a life aligned with your calling—not confined by roles, titles, or expectations that no longer fit. It's the freedom to choose meaningful work, to shift direction when your soul says it's time, and to define success on your own terms. This facet of wellness invites you to listen deeply to what lights you up and to honor your evolving sense of purpose. Purpose freedom is not about finding one fixed calling—it's about giving yourself the grace and space to follow what feels aligned in each season of your life.

Many people carry the limiting belief that purpose must be tied to productivity, career, or what others expect of them. We're taught to pick a path early and stick with it, even if it no longer fulfills us. This belief can keep us trapped in roles that look good on the outside but feel hollow on the inside. Whether out of obligation, fear, or the desire for approval, we end up performing purpose rather than living it—disconnected from what truly brings us joy, meaning, or a sense of contribution.

A more liberating belief is this: "My purpose is allowed to evolve, and I am free to follow what calls me now."

Purpose freedom begins when we release the pressure to have it all figured out and start paying attention to what energizes and sustains us. It's about honoring the quiet nudges, the inner shifts, and the sacred rest stops along the way. When we choose alignment over approval, we create a life that's not just successful, but soulful. In doing so, we reclaim our right to live with passion, intention, and a sense of deep fulfillment.

Journaling prompt: *Does how I spend my energy reflect what matters most to me? If not, what's one small way I can move closer to a life aligned with my current calling or curiosity?*

Liberation isn't a destination—it's a daily practice. It's the ongoing decision to live in alignment with who you truly are, not who the world told you to be. These ten facets of freedom—emotional, mental, physical, financial, creative, spiritual, social, time, identity, and purpose—offer a new framework for navigating life with intention and authenticity. Together, they form a holistic vision of wellness that centers choice, alignment, and self-trust. When we reflect on each facet, we begin to see where we've been confined and where we are ready to break free.

These facets are not rules—they are invitations. Invitations to pause, to question, and to choose again. To ask yourself: What does emotional freedom look like for me today? Am I honoring my time, or giving it away without thought? Do I feel safe to evolve, to express, to rest? Each question becomes a mirror, showing us where we are living in alignment and where we may still be shrinking. And each answer becomes a compass, gently guiding us back to ourselves.

CHAPTER 8

THE LIFE YOU'RE SEEKING FREEDOM FOR

Early in your journey, you made time to dream and spend a day with your future Self in the life you were seeking freedom for—now you're here! Now it is time to be intentional about making your dream life a reality.

Over the next thirty days, allow yourself to gently explore your liberated Present Self. Use these prompts to reflect on the life you're growing into, one choice at a time.

WEEK 1: MEETING YOUR PRESENT SELF

Focus: Introducing the vision, establishing trust, and beginning to name the life you desire.

1. What does your Present Self want you to know about the life you're now in alignment with?
   Mantra: My future is not a fantasy—it is a remembering of what I deserve.
2. Where do you live—mentally, physically, and emotionally? What is the energy of your home, your mind, your environment?

Mantra: I am creating the conditions that make peace possible.

3. What habits and patterns have you released to become who you are today? What did you finally let go of—and what did it free up space for you to receive?
   Mantra: I do not have to carry what no longer belongs to me.

WEEK 2: LIVING THE LIBERATED LIFE

Focus: Routines, values, and rhythms that support sustainable freedom.

1. What does a nourishing weekday look like for you? What do you prioritize when no one is watching?
   Mantra: I choose a daily life that reflects my deepest values.
2. How do you make decisions—especially hard ones? What guides your choices? How do you implement TERMS?
   Mantra: I no longer rush—I respond with clarity and care.
3. What role does rest play in your life? How do you honor rest without guilt?
   Mantra: Rest is not a reward—it is a requirement.

WEEK 3: RELATIONSHIPS AND BOUNDARIES

Focus: Exploring Present Self's connections—with others, self, and purpose.

1. Who is in your village or tribe—and how do those relationships feel? What friendships, partnerships, or communities have you nurtured or released?
   Mantra: I am surrounded by relationships that honor my wholeness.

2. How do you maintain boundaries without apology or fear? What do you say no to with ease—and what does that "no" protect?
   Mantra: Every boundary I set is a door I open to peace.
3. How do you reconnect with yourself when you feel ungrounded? What practices or reminders help you come back home?
   Mantra: No matter how far I drift out of alignment, I can always return to myself.

WEEK 4: EMBODIMENT AND EXPANSION

Focus: Fully becoming—living in alignment, claiming joy, and moving forward.

1. What does it look and/or feel like when your Present Self experiences joy without guilt? How do you celebrate yourself? What brings you pleasure?
   Mantra: I am allowed to enjoy the life I've created.
2. How do you navigate setbacks or moments of doubt? What does resilience look like without self-betrayal?
   Mantra: Even in uncertainty, I remain aligned with who I am becoming.
3. What has surprised you the most about the journey to living a liberated life? What have you discovered along the way that you never expected—but deeply needed?
   Mantra: Becoming who I am meant to be has been worth every step.

Spending time with your future Self is not an exercise in fantasy—it is an intentional act of self-inquiry. It offers a framework for examining the gap between your current reality and the life you envision, while helping you identify the values, habits, and boundaries required to bridge that distance. By engaging in this month-long reflection, you are doing the work of personal alignment—clarifying not only what freedom looks like for you but also what it will take to sustain it. Let this practice serve as both a vision and a roadmap—one rooted in self-awareness, integrity, and the ongoing commitment to becoming who you are meant to be.

CHAPTER 9

FILL THE WELLS

We have spent this journey together uncovering the weight we carry—not just in our homes or schedules, but in our minds and hearts. We have explored the origins of our overwhelm, the limiting beliefs that keep us tethered to cycles of excess, and the ways in which we can begin to unburden ourselves. And now, as we arrive at this moment, one truth remains: Living with less is not about sacrifice—it's about intention.

To choose less is to choose more. More clarity. More peace. More alignment with the life we say we want. But this path is not about perfection. It is about practice. It is about showing up, again and again, and choosing what serves us over what depletes us.

Every day, from the moment we wake up to the time we go to bed, we make thousands of choices—some consciously, others almost reflexively. What time we rise, what we eat, whether we exercise, how we respond to challenges, and even how we speak to ourselves—each decision, no matter how small, shapes the course of our lives. Yet, many of us underestimate the immense power embedded in our ability to choose. We surrender our agency to habits, external expectations, or fear, not realizing that our choices determine whether we live a life of overwhelm or one of intentionality and freedom.

The ability to choose—to say yes or no, to agree or disagree, to stay the course or pivot—is a superpower. It is the force that transforms aspirations into reality, chaos into clarity, and obligations into purpose-driven action. By recognizing the power of our choices and cultivating the wisdom to make them intentionally, we reclaim control over our lives. This, at its core, is the essence of intentional living: curating a life aligned with our values, aspirations, and well-being.

Throughout our lives, the past will always be our most dedicated teacher. Just like the lessons we learn in school, where each subject is broken into modules to build upon our knowledge over time, so are the past teachable moments and seasons of our lives. Every blessing, every bump in the road, is designed to prepare us for what's next. And just as it was when we were younger students, there will always be times when we feel like we failed a test we thought we'd pass with flying colors.

When we see our actual results and experience the painful collateral damage, it is natural to feel disappointed. The regret of not paying attention more closely, for failing to see the correct choice, which now seems so obvious upon reflection. The guilt of knowing we were too cavalier with second chances or broke our boundaries, hoping the risk would be worth the reward. The shame of others knowing our shortcomings. Their silent judgment we fear makes for lively gossip whenever we're not around, which is why, if we are not careful, the past can become less of a teacher and more of a tyrant dictating our thoughts and every move.

There is nothing we can do to change our past decisions, and with few exceptions, there is nothing we can do to remedy the harm. But we can and should allow the past to do what it came to do: teach us. And we can only do that if we choose to let go of the weighted burden of carrying our past regrets.

Remember to give yourself grace.

Letting the past keep you in bondage and unable to move forward in your life is the exact opposite of what those lessons came to teach you. Rather, you endured and survived your past decisions to use them as tools for your future liberation. So commit to not letting the past weigh you down and, instead, use those experiences to guide your footsteps toward the life you want and deserve.

BEING FREE, STAYING FREE

There was a time when you longed for the life you are stepping into now.

You dreamed of peace.

You craved balance.

You yearned for a life that felt lighter, fuller, freer.

And now? You hold that freedom in your hands. But make no mistake—freedom is not self-sustaining. If you are not careful, the weight of old habits, outdated expectations, and lingering obligations will creep back in. Not because you have failed, but because that is the nature of a world that constantly demands more.

Which is why you must be intentional about choosing less.

Less overextending.

Less proving.

Less apologizing for putting yourself first.

You have already done the hardest part—breaking free. Now your work is to ensure you stay free.

And that requires a level of deliberate, unapologetic, unwavering intention that most people will never practice.

Remember your TERMS. You do not have limitless time. You do not have infinite energy. Your resources—mental, emotional, financial—are not bottomless. So from this moment forward, you must spend them wisely.

Ask yourself: Who and what is worthy of my time?

Not in a nice way. Not in a "I don't want to hurt anyone's feelings" way. But in a radical, honest, no-bullshit way. You have worked too hard to return to a life where you are drained, distracted, and depleted. The world will keep demanding your energy if you allow it.

So don't.

Intention means saying no more than you say yes.

It means prioritizing rest as much as you prioritize productivity.

It means choosing alignment over obligation—every single time. Because you cannot afford to spend your time and energy on things that do not nourish you. Not anymore.

Of course, not everyone will understand (or like) this new version of you. Some people will be confused by your boundaries. Some will be frustrated by your refusal to overextend yourself. Some will miss the old you—the one who sacrificed, accommodated, and made their lives easier at your own expense.

That is their burden to bear, not yours.

Intention means protecting your peace even when it disappoints others. It means choosing relationships that pour into you—not just the ones that demand from you. It means knowing that your liberated life will not be for everyone—but the people who matter will celebrate it with you.

Remember: You cannot be free if you are unwell. Liberation means caring for yourself with the same devotion you once reserved for others. It means listening to your body before it has to scream for rest. It means moving through life with presence, joy, and ease—not just survival.

Because what is the point of building a life that feels good on the outside if it depletes you on the inside?

Your well-being is not a luxury. It is not something you tend to after you've handled everything else. It is the foundation of your freedom.

And if you are not intentional about protecting it, you will find yourself right back where you started.

Here's what happens when you are overly concerned about whether or not people like you. You cannot authentically live in your truth because you are constantly wondering whether or not the decision you make that may be best for you will cause others to dislike you, which is why it's so important and necessary to be okay with being disliked. Even by people in perceived positions of power. *Especially* by people in perceived positions of power. This is largely because people in positions of power, real or imagined, are rarely challenged or held accountable for their actions. Not because they are above reproach. But rather because others fear retaliation or repercussions such as being disliked, missing out on opportunities, or being ousted from a coveted position or community. We can understand both perspectives, yet choose not to remain in situations or dynamics that require a culture of silence.

To believe that your success is dependent on whether or not someone else likes you or is available to support you is a very limiting thought and belief, even from a spiritual perspective. The idea that the God source you serve would only allow you to be rewarded and blessed by not being your authentic self in the hopes of being liked is just counterintuitive to what faith actually means. You must have faith that whatever is meant for you is meant for you irrespective of persons with perceived or actual power who may appear to be standing in the way or be a threat or a hindrance. And most importantly you have to have faith in yourself.

Let people do whatever they want to do. Let them say whatever they want to say, and believe whatever they want to believe. There will always be people who have decided or determined that, for whatever reason, they don't like you. And that's okay! The less time you spend in relationships and in community with people who don't align with who you are and how you've changed, the more time you'll have for people who do.

YOUR LIBERATED LIFE STARTS NOW

This is it. This is the moment you step fully into the life you have been working toward.

You are no longer who you were before. You are no longer shackled to the expectations, beliefs, or obligations that once held you back.

You are free.

And the only thing standing between you and staying free is your intention.

So be intentional.

Be unwavering.

Be selfish when you need to be.

Be relentless in protecting the life you fought to create.

Because this—a life of clarity, alignment, and peace—is what you deserve.

And from now on? You will accept nothing less.

THE NECESSITY OF JOY

You made the commitment to find freedom from your life of overwhelm and you followed through. Congratulations! And indeed, we have saved the best for last—the necessities for cultivating the life you are seeking freedom for.

I still recall how I felt in the Sahara Desert, as I sat against the backdrop of a bright Moroccan mid-morning sun and realized that I not only felt free, *I was free.* I recall screaming as we raced dune buggies across the golden sand, the anticipation of riding to the top of the sand dune and being unable to see the drop awaiting me on the other side. How wonderful, how beautiful to just be one and at one with nature.

That trip was pivotal for me and it came at a pivotal time in my liberation journey. I'd just experienced the loss of someone who was a dear friend, like the older sister I'd always wanted. It was a necessary loss but devastating nonetheless, and the ripple effects could be felt throughout our shared community. Between grieving this loss and the impending deadline for this book, I'd strongly considered canceling my trip to Morocco.

That day, as all my Wells returned to optimal levels, I was so glad I hadn't.

That day, I realized the journey that I thought I'd been on for the past several months had actually been in progress for nearly three years. I thought about the time I'd spent in solitude—first by circumstance due to the pandemic and later by choice as an empty nester. How I'd grieved so many necessary losses and saw the end of so many transactional relationships. How I'd learned to embrace selfishness and surrender to the feelings that once held me captive. How I'd learned to finally implement TERMS and be protective of my most valuable asset: me.

This journey had led me to truly love and honor myself, and I felt so proud, so unbelievably proud! And more than anything, I felt joy. The most unexplainable, indescribable joy. And I knew it was not just my freedom from overwhelm but also because I was well. Thanks to my daily activities, healthy meals, scream-worthy adventures, fellow travelers who'd become friends, and, of course, my writing, I was at optimal wellness. That was what I felt: being well.

You've filled all your Wells, girl.

Indeed, I had.

And I knew I'd never let them be depleted again.

ROUTINES AND RITUALS FOR LIBERATION

Surely if I'd stayed in Morocco on my carefully curated trip by Camp Yoshi, my Wells would have stayed full. But alas, I had to come home, which meant it was going to require more effort to keep my Wells at optimal levels. I would have to be intentional.

I would have to be intentional about exercising, getting adequate rest, and so on.

Ultimately, I developed rituals and routines to ensure I not only stayed free from overwhelm but also stayed well.

Establishing routines and rituals are two of the best ways to ensure you enjoy your newfound freedom and stay the course on the life you were seeking freedom for. When we stop living life on autopilot, we get to exercise the power we worked so hard to reclaim. Now that we are in control, it is our responsibility to be intentional about how we navigate our days. And we do this by being intentional about how we manage our time, energy, relationships, and resources.

Our liberatory routines and rituals are how we make honoring our TERMS a daily practice.

routine[1]

noun. a sequence of actions regularly followed; a fixed program

ritual[2]

noun. a sequence of activities involving gestures, words, actions, or revered objects

Routines are how we structure our days. Rituals are the special ways in which we choose to honor our days and ourselves.

Please note that the following routines and rituals are merely examples of structuring my life in ways that worked for *me.*

Among the many things we have learned on our journey, we know that we cannot have a "one size fits all" approach to life. Feel free to modify what I have shared or use these suggestions as a guide to create your own liberatory routines and rituals to manage your blessings. The goal is to establish a lifestyle where you are intentional about caring for your Personal Wells and overall well-being.

Remember: Our bodies are always, *always* trying to be well, and more importantly, stay well. The least we can do is have rituals and routines that support this goal.

You may be unsure of where or how to cultivate a ritual to honor your Personal Wells. I recall feeling the same, particularly because I was just learning how to trust myself. Quite a few of my early "honor the Wells" rituals had a way of making me *over* course-correct! Since then, I have learned to keep my daily rituals simple and straightforward.

A DAILY ROUTINE

A Good Day Starts the Night Before

Although I am still a member of the 5 a.m. Club,* I no longer have the same routine that once governed my mornings. There was a time when I used to wake up at 5 a.m. (sometimes a little earlier), head straight to the kitchen to make coffee, and then straight to my computer to start working. The goal was to get as much done as possible before the rest of the world woke up and began making demands.

---

* This is not an actual club but rather a common classification for people who wake up at 5 a.m. to start their day. The concept comes from the book *The 5 AM Club* by Robin Sharma.

Oy!

These days, my early mornings are different and much more easeful. And I will let you in on the secret as to why: How I manage my mornings as well as each day starts the night before.

When our days are full, we often find ourselves saying, "I'll do it tomorrow." However, when tomorrow comes, there isn't enough time or space to fit in whatever "it" is. And the feelings of overwhelm begin to loom.

Because rarely do we have as much time as we think we do.

An easy routine to ensure your days aren't unnecessarily overwhelming is to review your schedule the night before. This is more than looking at what is on the agenda. It is an honest self-assessment of your availability *and* capacity.

Set the Scene

Be relaxed and comfortable. This will allow you to listen to your body more easily. How does your body react to what will be required of you to get through tomorrow?

Assess the Wells

Check in to see how you are feeling physically, emotionally, mentally, socially, and spiritually. Are you tired or hungry? Do you need to cry? Are you mentally exhausted? Are you feeling supported by your community? Does your work feel meaningful?

Honor the Wells

This is the moment of truth: Is there anything that you no longer have the capacity to take on? If so, prepare your canned "Unfortunately, I need to reschedule or cancel" message so that you can send it to recipients first thing in the morning.

Fill the Wells

Ensure your day includes dedicated moments and activities that fill your Personal Wells.

Preparing for tomorrow the night before is a routine that allows you to navigate your days without the element of surprise each morning. Of course, there will always be unexpected obligations and responsibilities that arise, which is all the more reason to know in advance what each day will bring, so you can better manage the occasional overwhelm to ensure it does not become constant.

One of the simplest rituals to ensure I am honoring my wellness (and myself) is what I have coined the 3Ps: pause, proceed, or pivot.

A DAILY RITUAL

I Feel, I Am

When overwhelm is our baseline, we have a tendency to say "I feel" as opposed to "I am." Unfortunately, over time, we've learned to disregard and push aside our feelings for the sake of getting things. So we no longer "hear" what our feelings are trying to tell us.

It took me a few weeks before I could recognize what I was embodying. Here is the strategy that worked best for me: Whenever I found myself saying "I feel . . ." I repeated the sentence and replaced the word "feel" with "am."

You're more likely to get something to eat if you say "I am hungry" versus "I feel hungry."

You're more likely to understand that your body needs rest if you say "I am tired" versus "I feel tired."

You're more likely not to go out if you say "I am socially drained" versus "I feel socially drained."

Remember, the ultimate goal of personal liberation is learning to honor who we are as opposed to how we feel.

THE 3Ps RITUAL

Step 1: Pause

At the end of your day, whether before your nightly routine or as the last activity before bedtime, think about what is on your agenda the next day. It may help to look at your calendar to see what professional meetings or personal meetups are scheduled and if any deliverables are due.

Pause to check in with yourself and the capacity of your Personal Wells. How does looking at tomorrow's responsibilities and obligations make you feel? Are your feelings of overwhelm temporary or circumstantial? Does the day seem manageable or overwhelming?

Honoring your Personal Wells means being honest with yourself. When you pause, you are taking a moment to self-assess and determine whether you have the capacity to move through your scheduled day as planned.

Step 2: Proceed or Pivot

Based on your honest assessment, decide whether to proceed with your day as planned or pivot to adjusting.

Depending on the circumstances, you may be able to pivot immediately. For example, you could text a friend you were planning to have lunch with to express regrets that you'll have to reschedule because you're overcommitted. Other times, it may be best for you to pivot and make adjustments early in the workday to cancel or reschedule a meeting. Regardless of when and how you decide to communicate your need to pivot, acknowledging that you need to make adjustments the night before ensures that you will start the next day honoring your Personal Wells.

Beware of the Trifecta

Step 1 of 3 Ps ritual—pause—is a highly effective way to help you identify where and when you need to do less, which means it is also highly likely that you will have to face the trifecta of feelings when you choose to pivot. Remember to surrender to whatever you are feeling:

The *guilt* of having to cancel or reschedule.
The *shame* of having to admit you do not have the bandwidth.
The fear of whether you might *regret* your decision.

Otherwise, you risk reluctantly proceeding and finding yourself overwhelmed, which, ironically, will lead to the trifecta of feelings as well—you will feel the guilt, shame, and regret for not honoring yourself.

You may find yourself using the 3Ps ritual in a variety of ways to honor yourself and your wellness. It is a great way to start cultivating rituals that help you regularly self-assess your overall well-being and hold yourself accountable to choose less if and whenever you need to.

AN ANNUAL RITUAL

Lowest Lows, Highest Highs

Whether you know it or not, can see it or not, or have already experienced it or not—our lowest lows have a way of leading us to our highest highs. Physically. Emotionally. Mentally. Socially. Spiritually. Everything you had to let go has made space for more of what you need and deserve. Everyone you had to part ways with has made space for genuine connections and the love your heart desires. Every hardship already has or will soon help you heal. Every great loss already has or will soon help you grow.

When I say "Choose less. Be free. Be well," I mean this statement literally. I mean, this is a strategy that can not only change your life—it can also save it.

Whenever we choose *more*—to do, to have, to be responsible for—we have less time and energy to care for ourselves. Whenever we choose *less*—to do, to have, to be responsible for—we have more personal freedom to focus on our overall well-being.

Choosing less—to stop people-pleasing, to stop doing the most—afforded me more time to prioritize my health and healing.

Being free—spending more time in nature, learning to surrender and release every emotion bottled inside—is how I cared for myself and my overall well-being.

Being well—being fully committed to strengthening my physical, emotional, mental, social, and spiritual health—is what I had to do to survive.

Sometimes, we have to press pause on fighting for collective liberation so we can save ourselves.

Freedom is more than a premise—it is a personal commitment. Because collective liberation begins with Self. *We* must honor our longings for liberation before we can help others get free. *We* must embody personal liberation to show others that we are here for more than a life of doing.

We are here for a life of being.

I believe our *lowest lows* are always trying to lead us to our *highest highs*. But if we are constantly overwhelmed by doing, we can miss the lessons. And if we are unwell, we can miss the blessings.

Throughout my journey, I thought a lot about how the work of liberation has become commodified. How it is so sweetly packaged, shiny and attractive, sellable, which is why we often find ourselves in disbelief when it feels like our entire world is crumbling. To be clear and fair, it is crumbling. Lesson after lesson. Loss after loss. The work, your work, is to rebuild it.

Moment after moment. Day after day. Season after season. Milestone after milestone.

It will feel like this work is never-ending. But you will be too far ahead in your journey to go back to where you started. And you may feel that you are nowhere close to the life you want and deserve. (It will feel that way, but trust me—you're closer than you think!) It is in these moments that it is an absolute necessity to cultivate moments of joy.

Yes, even in the hardest of times. Especially in the hardest of times.

Remember: The work of healing yourself, the work of honoring yourself, is in and of itself worthy of celebration.

It may seem counterintuitive, but one of the best ways to cultivate joy is by first surrendering to the uncomfortable feelings you are facing. Yell. Scream. Rage. Weep. Let it all out.

Trust me, this was not a technique for finding joy that I actually cultivated, not at first. Like many high points on my journey, I stumbled upon it by happenstance. One early morning, when I was convinced I'd made a mess of my life trying to find freedom from overwhelm, I decided to write a letter to myself.

Dear Christine,

You have been through a lot in this lifetime . . . and it's okay.

You are learning to accept the truth, about yourself and others . . . and it's okay.

You are learning to surrender . . . and it's okay.

You are learning to let go . . . and it's okay.

You are learning to grieve . . . and it's okay.

You are learning to forgive yourself . . . and it's okay.

You are learning to honor yourself . . . and it's okay.

You are learning to love yourself . . . and it's okay.

As I read it aloud to myself, I could feel emotions starting to rise to the surface. Not that I'd been trying to suppress them—I certainly cried more than my fair share of tears. But whatever this was, it was something different. So I kept writing.

Dear Christine,

You will survive.

This season is not like the average season, one that comes and goes with distinct shifts and changes letting me know that it has come to an end. No, this season is long and hard, and it seems never-ending. But I just keep telling myself . . . you will survive.

This season it seems I've made a mess of life. A mess of myself. A mess of my work. A mess of friendships. A mess of love, of trying to love and receiving love. But I just keep telling myself . . . you will survive.

This season came so unexpectedly, so sudden and sweeping. Hardship after hardship. Heartbreak after heartbreak. Disappointment after disappointment. Loss after loss. But I just keep telling myself . . . you will survive.

This season has brought me to my knees. Rocked me to my core. Shaken everything. Taken everything. I truly have nothing left to give. But I just keep telling myself . . . you will survive.

This season, when it ends, as all seasons must do, I will shout. I will scream. I will laugh. I will cry. I will rejoice that my suffering has ended.

I will let the world know that I did indeed survive.

Oh, that one did it. In that moment, it felt like my soul cracked open and every memory, every emotion that had seen me through the journey poured out. I cried. Not the ugly cries I had daily. This one was quieter, softer. A true surrender. Only when it ended did I realize what I'd been holding in, the feeling I'd been refusing to release: defeat.

My entire world and all my Personal Wells had been turned inside out and upside down, and there I was standing in the mess of it all, alone with no one to help or hold me. I felt defeated. Absolutely and utterly humiliated. Broken-spirited and brokenhearted. Everything seemed beyond repair. This journey had been the longest season of my life . . . and it still hadn't ended.

But nothing, nothing lasts forever, right?

Every day, every single day, I tell myself: This is but one small moment on the timeline of your big life. For I know this to be true. I absolutely, positively know this to be true. Even though it seems like the largest lie.

Every day, every single day, I tell myself: This is the day that it's going to end. The storm is over! Weeping has endured for nights and nights, and this is the morning that joy is coming. Alas, it has yet to ring true. Alas, it seems like the largest lie.

Every day, every single day, I tell myself: Just keep going, just keep believing, just keep trying, just keep pushing through. And I do, I do. Regardless of feeling like I'm making no progress at all, I do. Even though life seems like the largest lie.

Every day, every single day, I tell myself: In one year, in five years, in ten years . . . will you even remember this moment that seemed larger than life itself? Will you remember it as a time that nearly swallowed you whole? Or will you speak of it as the time that defined and refined you?

One day, every single day, you will tell others how the most treacherous journey led you to freedom.

I wrote that poem as my tears dried. My eyes were so swollen, I remember squinting to see as I typed the words into Notes on my phone. And with each refrain, I began to feel a new emotion start to arise: joy.

It was an unexpected release.

You are likely reading this book almost one year, five years, or perhaps ten years or more from the day I wrote these poems on January 6, 2025—the day I turned in my first full manuscript for *Less Is Liberation.*

Since that day, I remain intentional about cultivating moments of joy—in both seasons of hardship and not. Of giving thanks each day when I wake up. Of savoring the smell of freshly brewed coffee. Of morning walks in the spring and summer, and evening strolls in fall and winter.

Smile at the babies that scowl, who look at you with complete distrust despite their mother's urging. Laugh at the way your face looks, your clothes look, your house looks—everything about you in need of proper care—as you stumble through the thick of it. Dance, a ridiculous, embarrassing dance, alone but even better if others are watching.

Call the friend that makes you laugh until you cry. Go out to dinner with the friend who makes you howl so loud, you always wonder not if but when you'll get kicked out of a restaurant. Say hello to a kind stranger. Stop to talk to a senior who looks like they haven't had a good conversation in a while.

The next time it rains, step outside and allow yourself to get wet. Drenched. Then sing as loud as you can, so loud and so free that people passing by can't help but smile. Splash in the puddles. Make angels in the snow. And if you're ever driving a dune buggy across the golden sands of the Sahara Desert, scream and laugh and allow yourself to be joyful.

Joy will nourish you as you do the inner work to honor your commitment to finding freedom from your life of overwhelm. Joy will sustain you as you continue your journey building the intentional life you've spent so much time longing for. You have honored that longing for freedom, *your* longing for freedom, and you will be rewarded.

There is an opportunity to experience joy, absolute joy, in every moment of every day. We just have to choose to see it. And when we do, that is our sign, a way for our bodies to let us know that liberation is always, *always* attainable.

We are always, *always* but one loss, one lesson, one love, one laugh away from finding freedom for the lives we want and deserve.

May you choose less.

May you be free.

May you be well.

Today, and forevermore.

A DAILY PRACTICE TO CENTER AND HONOR YOURSELF

Far too often we say that we "don't have time" for ourselves. But the reality is that we do! We simply have not made being chiefly concerned with ourselves and our well-being a practice or a priority. One way to start being unapologetically selfish is by making centering and honoring yourself a daily practice. Start your day with this fifteen-minute routine to begin the beautiful work of learning how to be intentional about the care and keeping of you.

Ground Yourself in Stillness (three minutes)

Before reaching for your phone or jumping into the day, take a moment to simply be.

Sit or lie down with your eyes closed. Feel the weight of your body, the rhythm of your breath, and the presence of this moment.

Breathe into Your Body (three minutes)

Practice a simple breathwork exercise to connect with yourself. Inhale for four counts, hold for four counts, exhale for six counts. Repeat for three minutes, allowing each exhale to release tension and create space for your needs.

Check In with Yourself (three minutes)

Place a hand on your heart or belly and ask: What do I need less of today? What do I need more of today? Where can I give myself grace? Listen to your answers without judgment. Honor these truths as guidance, not demands.

Set Your Intention for the Day (three minutes)

Gently ask yourself: What do I need today? or How do I want to feel? Let your answer guide you. Your intention can be a single word (ease, joy, strength) or a short affirmation ("I honor my needs today" or "My energy is sacred").

Commit to One Small Act of Honoring Yourself (three minutes)

Choose one small way to prioritize yourself today. It could be as simple as drinking water before coffee, taking a deep breath before answering a message, or pausing before saying yes to a request. Small, mindful choices add up to a life of self-honoring.

AFTERWORD

As I write this afterword, I am sitting in a cabin overlooking Harvey's Lake in the Poconos of Pennsylvania. And I am literally *sitting* in a cabin, a two-story A-frame with wood paneling that I rented out to spend spring break weekend with my now-twenty-one-year-old daughter. She is composing music for her senior recital while I am composing the ending to this book that chronicled what I now know was my rite of passage: separation, liminality, and only recently, reintegration. Because in this moment, as I sit with yet another new core memory, I not only feel free, I realize that *I am free*.

Earlier today, a dear friend sent me an Instagram DM—which nowadays, amid so much political and socioeconomic strife that people are too overwhelmed and overcome with worries, is akin to sending a long text message with heart emojis. Michell and I haven't talked in a few days, and this is her way of saying, "I miss you. And I love you."

Smiling, I tapped the image directing me to a stranger's post. Smiling because whether I am about to see shenanigans or something serious, it made my friend think of me. As I listened, I realized the video was the latter, something serious. So I turned up the volume to listen closely to a Black woman staring intently into the camera.

"Did you know why some flamingos' feathers turn white?" she asked. "I didn't even know they could lose their pink coloring!"

Me neither.

"But that's what happens when they are so worn-out and depleted from tending to their young. From just . . . wearing themselves out. And it made me think: I need to get my pink back."

Tears well in my eyes. For many reasons. For the many seasons my limiting beliefs caused me to lose my vibrancy, when I was constantly overwhelmed and depleted from giving more of myself than I ever had or needed to give. I cry for the years I spent people-pleasing—platonically, romantically, and collegially. The wound of feeling used is still healing, there is a small scab where there was once a gaping hole. And I tap my heart like the healers taught me, to release the last of the pain I'm harboring and to honor what I have survived.

I sob when I think of the last cords being cut, of the last soul ties being severed. It is hard to let go of transactional relationships that you poured yourself into, believing there was reciprocity. Believing your love alone was strong enough to make a connection genuine. I let out a wail, a primal cry that does not even sound like it belongs to me. But I know the pain being screamed into a pillow wet with tears is indeed mine. Because few things are harder to grieve than those you love who are still among the living.

I wrap my arms around myself. Pulling myself closer, hugging myself tighter. Because I am so proud of myself for doing the inner work to get my pink back.

Motherhood softened all my hard edges. Taught me a level of patience I did not know was possible. I learned to be everything and everyone I needed to be to raise, nurture, teach, and care for another human being (which is so much harder than people think it is!). I gave motherhood my all . . . which left me with very little for myself. And in time, being self-sacrificing to the point of overwhelm became my baseline.

By the time my daughter went off to college, I'd become a flamingo. A woman who had been so self-sacrificing for so long, I did not even realize that it had become a part of my identity. Even though I was an empty nester, I kept finding someone, something, *anything* to pour into to feel worthy, to feel validated, to feel loved. I continued to give of myself to the point of overwhelm . . . and life sent me into a season of separation.

I wish someone had told me that we encounter many rites of passage in our lifetime. Perhaps, if we knew such things, we would allow ourselves to pause and be present. Perhaps, we would not be so tempted to rush through life transitions; maybe we would take the time to learn and appreciate what they have come to show and teach us about the beautiful complexity of humanhood.

The birth of children. Those who made it earthside, and those that occurred in a sacred place with rainbows who were birthed within our hearts.

The death of loved ones. Those that were expected, those that were unexpected. For there is nothing like the grief of having to say goodbye. And yet again, we must think of parents and their children. For there is nothing worse than having to grieve someone who you birthed or nurtured from the womb of another.

The strange feeling of estrangement. For there is a different type of grief for the loss of loved ones who are still living.

The love so beautiful, so sacred, so once-in-a-lifetime that it causes anticipatory grief.

The love so painful, so awful, so dangerous that it causes us nothing but despair.

Our engagements. Our marriages. Our divorces.

Our friends who were once like family members who we no longer claim.

The jobs and careers that we never thought would end.

The financial struggles that leave us strapped or lead to insolvency.

The diagnoses and diseases that cause us to face our own mortality.

There are so many personal rites of passage we encounter in our lifetimes. But rarely do we allow ourselves to enter them fully. Rarely do we allow ourselves to fully experience what a rite of passage has come to teach us about ourselves and others. Instead, we stay in a constant state of overwhelm and misalignment, continuing to push through instead of pausing to honor these sacred seasons of our lives. While the inner work is not always easy, it is always available, always accessible, and its goal is always, *always* for us to be well.

We must simply learn to be intentional about honoring ourselves.

May you choose less. May you be free. May you be well.

May you always remember that you are the road that leads to freedom from your life of overwhelm.

ACKNOWLEDGMENTS

This is certainly the shortest acknowledgments I've ever written—indeed, less *is* liberation!

To my agents, Jordan Hill and Jo Volpe at New Leaf Media & Literary, thank you for your unwavering belief in both my message and my voice. To my editor, Nana Twumasi, and the entire publishing team at GCP Balance, I am forever grateful for your care, clarity, and commitment to helping me bring this project to life. Words aren't ever enough to express my appreciation.

To my mother, daughter, closest friends, literary coconspirators, and allies—you know who you are—thank you for holding me through the quiet, uncertain seasons of liminality. Your presence gave me the strength to keep going, even on the days when I wasn't sure I could. Thank you for being my chrysalis as I grew wings and learned to fly.

And to every place that held me while I healed—Washington, DC; Morocco; New York; Pennsylvania; Virginia; West Virginia; and Spain—thank you for the space, the stillness, and the gifts of sweet surrender. *Less Is Liberation* would not exist without the love and care you've shown me.

May we all enjoy the lives we are seeking freedom for.

NOTES

INTRODUCTION

1. "Black Baby Girls More Likely to Live When Born Very Premature," *ScienceDaily*, January 4, 2006, https://www.sciencedaily.com/releases/2006/01/060103183741.htm.

2. Elana Dure, "Black Women Are the Fastest Growing Group of Entrepreneurs. But the Job Isn't Easy," J.P. Morgan, October 12, 2021, https://www.jpmorgan.com/insights/business-planning/black-women-are-the-fastest-growing-group-of-entrepreneurs-but-the-job-isnt-easy.

3. "Fast Facts: Women of Color in Higher Ed," AAUW, accessed May 1, 2025, https://www.aauw.org/resources/article/fast-facts-woc-higher-ed/.

4. Nadrea R. Njoku and Lori D. Patton, "Persistence and Resistance: Black Women Navigating Barriers in Higher Education," Century Foundation, September 12, 2003, https://tcf.org/content/report/persistence-and-resistance-black-women-navigating-barriers-in-higher-education/.

5. Ruhama Wolle, "The Unwavering Black Women Voters," *Glamour*, September 5, 2024, https://www.glamour.com/story/election-2024-the-unwavering-black-women-voters.

CHAPTER 1

1. Ella L. J. Edmondson Bell and Stella M. Nkomo, *Our Separate Ways: Black and White Women and the Struggle for Professional Identity* (Harvard Business School Press, 2001).

2. Bell and Nkomo, *Our Separate Ways.*

3. Megan Dalla-Camina, "How to Deal with Overwhelm," *Psychology Today*, April 26, 2023, https://www.psychologytoday.com/us/blog/real-women/202303/how-to-deal-with-overwhelm.

4. Albert Bandura, *Self-efficacy: The Exercise of Control* (W. H. Freeman, 1997).

5. John G. Cottone, "Gen Z Takes on Mental Health," *Psychology Today*, January 11, 2025, https://www.psychologytoday.com/us/blog/the-cube/2024 05/gen-z-takes-on-mental-health.

6. Cottone, "Gen Z Takes on Mental Health."

7. Cottone, "Gen Z Takes on Mental Health."

8. Raju J. Das, Capital, Capitalism and Health," *Critical Sociology* 49, no. 3 (May 2023): 395–414.

9. Arline T. Geronimus, *Weathering: The Extraordinary Stress of Ordinary Life in an Unjust Society* (Little, Brown Spark, 2023).

10. Larissa Calancie et al., "Racial Disparities in Stroke Incidence in the Women's Health Initiative: Exploring Biological, Behavioral, Psychosocial, and Social Risk Factors," *SSM–Population Health* 25, no. 4 (December 2023): 101570.

11. "Unwell," *Merriam-Webster's Collegiate Dictionary*, accessed September 12, 2024, https://www.merriam-webster.com/dictionary/unwell.

12. Eterna Integrative website, accessed March 26, 2025, https://www .eternaintegrative.com/.

CHAPTER 2

1. Amanda Musa, "Experts Explain Phenomenon of Adults Who Leave Their Lives Behind," CNN, December 15, 2024, https://edition.cnn.com /2024/12/15/us/missing-persons-cases-runaways/index.html.

2. Francisco Garcia, "When Missing People Don't Want to Be Found," *The Guardian*, June 5, 2021, https://www.theguardian.com/lifeandstyle/2021/jun /05/when-missing-people-dont-want-to-be-found-id-removed-myself-to-push -world-away.

3. Garcia, "When Missing People Don't Want to Be Found."

4. Silvi Saxena, "Avoidance Behavior: Examples, Impacts, & How to Overcome," Choosing Therapy, September 20, 2024, https://www.choosing therapy.com/avoidance-behavior/.

5. Consensus Conference Panel, "Recommended Amount of Sleep for a Healthy Adult," *Sleep* 1, no. 38 (June 2015): 843–44.

6. Yasmin Anwar, "Emoji Fans Take Heart: Scientists Pinpoint 27 States of Emotion," UC Berkeley News, September 6, 2017, https://news.berkeley .edu/2017/09/06/27-emotions/.

7. Ella Zeigler, "'The Totally Not Boring Book of Feelings' Now Available for Purchase," BYU-Idaho Radio, September 3, 2024, https://www.byui.edu /radio/the-totally-not-boring-book-of-feelings-now-available-for-purchase.

8. "U.S. Adults Score on Par with International Average in Literacy Skills, Below International Average in Numeracy and Problem-Solving Skills in Survey of Adult Skills," National Center for Education Statistics, December 10, 2024, https://nces.ed.gov/whatsnew/press_releases/12_10_2024.asp.

9. Jeffrey Gaines, "The Philosophy of Ikigai: 3 Examples About Finding Purpose," Positive Psychology, November 17, 2020, https://positivepsychology.com/ikigai/.

10. Gaines, "Philosophy of Ikigai."

11. Erin Blakemore, "How the Daughter of a Slave Became the First African-American Woman to Earn a Bachelor's Degree," Time.com, May 23, 2017, https://time.com/4788672/mary-jane-patterson-history/

12. Blakemore, "Daughter of a Slave."

13. Blakemore, "Daughter of a Slave."

CHAPTER 3

1. Yvette Alt Miller, "Emma Lazarus, the Jews and Israel," aish.com, accessed May 1, 2025, https://aish.com/emma-lazarus-the-jews-and-israel/#:~:text=Her%20series%20would%20eventually%20grow,homeward%20to%20its%20ancient%20source%E2%80%9D.

CHAPTER 6

1. "Selfish," *Merriam-Webster's Collegiate Dictionary*, accessed September 12, 2024, https://www.merriam-webster.com/dictionary/selfish.

2. "Selfish."

3. "Resilience," *Merriam-Webster's Collegiate Dictionary*, accessed September 12, 2024, https://www.merriam-webster.com/dictionary/resilience.

4. D. Fletcher and M. Sarkar, "Psychological Resilience: A Review and Critique of Definitions, Concepts, and Theory," *European Psychologist* 18, no. 1 (2013): 12–23.

5. Mark Travers, "A Psychologist Explains Why You Shouldn't Be Afraid To Say 'No,'" Forbes.com, October 5, 2024, https://www.forbes.com/sites/traversmark/2024/10/05/a-psychologist-explains-why-you-shouldnt-be-afraid-to-say-no/.

CHAPTER 9

1. "Routine," *Oxford Dictionary*, accessed May 1, 2025, https://www.oed.com/dictionary/routine.

2. "Ritual," *Oxford Dictionary*, accessed May 1, 2025, https://www.oed.com/dictionary/ritual_adj?tab=factsheet#25076562.

INDEX

agency, 74–75
alignment
  boundaries and, 130, 131
  financial freedom and, 141
  identity freedom and, 146
  intention and, 156
  limiting beliefs and, 51, 94
  loss and, 106
  mental freedom and, 139
  overwhelm and, 22–24, 176
  personal freedom and, 70, 71, 136–137, 157, 158
  physical freedom and, 140
  purpose freedom and, 147
  self-assessments, 96–97, 149, 151, 152
  spiritual freedom and, 142
  time freedom and, 145
  wellness and, 49, 51–52, 61, 70, 71, 72, 73, 74
altruism, 16
American Dream, 28–29, 30
Angelou, Maya, 36
annual ritual, 165–171
anticipatory grief, 5–6, 112, 175
authority figures, 26, 27, 121
avoidance behaviors, 47–48

baby boom generation, 18, 28–29, 129
Beadle, Esther, 46–47
Beyoncé, 36
Black women, 6–11
  fear experienced by, 8
  wealth and earning power of, 7–8
  See also Love Notes to Black women
boundaries
  agency and, 74
  costs of breaking, 154
  financial freedom and, 141
  protecting Personal Wells and, 117–118, 119, 129–130
  relationships and, 150–151, 156
  social freedom and, 144

capitalism, 20, 37
Cheyenne, Yasmine, 39
community, 54–55. *See also* Social Well
Cook, Lauren, 47
COVID-19 pandemic, 5–6, 34, 55, 63, 159
creative freedom, 141–142

daily practice to center and honor yourself, 171–172
daily ritual, 163–164
daily routine, 161–163
Dead Prez, 125, 127
death, 112–116

depression, 37, 39, 40, 83, 104, 110
diaspora, African, 6, 123
disappear, urge to, 44–48, 61
divine guidance and connection, 4–5, 125, 142–143

Edmondson, Ella L. J., 19
emotional freedom, 137–138
Emotional Well, 41, 53, 57, 80, 96, 103. *See also* Personal Wells
empty nesters, 5, 34, 39, 159, 175
entrepreneurship, 9, 29

filling Personal Wells, 73, 86, 153–155
  annual ritual for, 165–171
  daily practice to center and honor yourself, 171–172
  daily ritual for, 163–164
  daily routine for, 161–163
  freedom and, 155–157
  intention and, 73, 153–161, 170–171, 172
  joy and, 158–159
  routines and rituals for, 159–172
  3Ps ritual for, 164–165
financial freedom, 140–141
first-generation achievements, 58–60
Five Foundations of Wellness, 40–41. *See also* Personal Wells
freedom, 3–4, 135–136
  creative freedom, 141–142
  emotional freedom, 137–138
  financial freedom, 140–141
  honoring our, 136–137
  identity freedom, 146
  inner work of, 71–75, 92–95, 97–98, 100
  intention and, 135, 136, 137, 139, 145, 147, 148
  mental freedom, 138–139
  mile markers to, 72–75
  other work of, 75
  physical freedom, 139–140
  purpose freedom, 147
  social freedom, 144
  spiritual freedom, 142–143
  time freedom, 145
Freedom From, Freedom For, 61–66, 72
Future Self exercise, 64–68, 149

Gemechisa, Gelane, 39–41, 84
Generation X, 18, 29–30, 43, 129
Generation Z, 31–32, 129
Geronimus, Arline T., 37
grief
  anticipatory grief, 5–6, 112, 175
  healing process and, 110–116
  necessity of, 110–112
grind culture, 20, 30, 89
guilt, 104

Hamer, Fannie Lou, 70
happiness, 51, 92–93, 103, 114
healing Personal Wells, 72–73, 101–116
  avoiding, 102
  grief and, 110–116
  guilt and, 104
  loss and, 106–110, 112–116
  regret and, 105
  shame and, 104–105
health and wellness
  aging and, 36–39
  emotional health, 40
  integrative health care, 39–41, 48
  mental and intellectual health, 40
  physical health, 40
  social health, 40–41
  spiritual health, 41
  See also Personal Wells; unwell, state of being
health disparities, 38
hip-hop, 124–125
Historical Well, 56–58, 63, 81, 98, 103. *See also* Personal Wells
honesty, 98, 102, 111, 138, 144
hooks, bell, 87

identity freedom, 146
ikigai, 56, 67
inner work, 71–75, 92–95, 97–98, 100

integrative health care, 39–41, 48
intention and intentional living, 4
  agency and, 74
  boundaries and, 131
  filling Personal Wells and, 73, 153–161, 170–171, 172
  freedom and, 135, 136, 137, 139, 145, 147, 148
  introspection and, 92
  self-care and, 38
  self-prioritizing and, 39
introspection, 71, 72, 90–100, 102, 117

Jim Crow policies, 19–20
journaling, 1, 42, 85, 95
journaling prompts
  creative freedom, 142
  emotional freedom, 138
  financial freedom, 141
  identity freedom, 146
  mental freedom, 139
  physical freedom, 140
  purpose freedom, 147
  social freedom, 144
  spiritual freedom, 143
  time freedom, 145
joy, 158–159

kindness, 98
King, Martin Luther, Jr., 70

Lazarus, Emma, 70
liberation. *See* freedom
limiting beliefs, 21, 24–27
  of baby boomers, 28–29
  creative freedom and, 142
  definition of, 24
  emotional freedom and, 138–139
  fear of change, 51
  financial freedom and, 141
  first-gen accomplishments and, 58–60
  freedom and, 43, 62, 69, 71
  of Generation X, 29–30
  of Generation Z, 31–32
  guilt, shame and regret, 103–105
  identity freedom and, 146
  introspection and, 90–94, 98–100
  loss and, 113
  of millennials, 30–31
  need for approval, 51
  need to be perfect, 50–51
  need to be productive, 51
  overwhelm and, 4–5, 7, 8
  physical freedom and, 140
  power of, 25–27
  purpose freedom and, 146
  self-sacrifice, 10, 25, 112, 119–120, 129, 175
  social freedom and, 144
  spiritual freedom and, 143
  state of being unwell and, 41–42
  time freedom and, 145
  well-being and, 50–52
  working twice as hard, 18–20
  See also people-pleasing
loss
  grief and, 112–116
  necessity of, 106–110
love languages, 106
Love Notes to Black women
  on deserving to be free and well, 76–77
  on first-gen achievement, 58–60
  on health and aging, 36–38
  on introspection, 93–94
  on loss, 108–109
  on purposeful pauses, 88–89
  on resilience, 123–124
  on stopping overwhelm, 9–11
  on working twice as hard, 18–20
Lululemon Community Coalition, 125–127

Malcolm X, 7
mental freedom, 138–139
Mental Well, 42, 48, 53–54, 55, 57, 80, 96. *See also* Personal Wells
millennial generation, 18, 30–31, 129
Morocco, 1–2, 64, 83–86, 101, 158–159
motherhood, 174–175
Musa, Amanda, 45

Nkomo, Stella M., 19

Oberlin College, 58
other work, 75. *See also* inner work
overachievement, 5, 60, 91
overcommitment, 5, 145, 164
overwhelm
 alignment and, 22–24, 176
 definition of, 22
 limiting beliefs and, 4–5, 7, 8
 Love Notes to Black women, 9–11
 normalizing, 76–77
 state of being unwell and, 9–11, 48
 See also limiting beliefs

pandemic. *See* COVID-19 pandemic
patience, 75, 98–99, 174
Patterson, Mary Jane, 58
Pendleton, Samantha, 107
people-pleasing, 5, 17, 20, 25, 35, 91, 135
 costs of, 33, 62, 83, 126, 129, 157, 174
 healing and stopping, 64, 101, 106–107, 112, 124, 166
 loss and, 106–107, 112
Personal Wells, 41–42, 43, 48–49, 52–58, 61
 assessing, 72, 83–95, 96–97
 Emotional Well, 41, 53, 57, 80, 96, 103
 Historical Well, 56–58, 63, 81, 98, 103
 Mental Well, 42, 48, 53–54, 55, 57, 80, 96
 mile markers of, 72–73
 Personal Wells Performance Evaluation, 94–95, 96–97
 Physical Well, 41, 52–53, 57, 80, 96
 routines and rituals, 161, 163, 164
 Social Well, 42, 54–55, 57, 80, 96
 Spiritual Well, 42, 55–56, 57, 81, 96–97
 See also filling Personal Wells; healing Personal Wells; protecting Personal Wells
physical freedom, 139–140
Plutchik, Robert, 53
Present Self exercise, 149–152
problem-solving skills, 40, 54, 142
productivity, 30–31, 33, 51, 92–93, 96, 156
protecting Personal Wells, 73, 86, 117–131
 boundaries and, 117–118, 119, 129–130
 resilience and, 121–123
 selfishness and, 117–124, 129–130
 setting terms for, 124–131
 TERMS (time, energy, relationships, money, sanity), 128–130
 ways to say no, 130–131
purpose freedom, 147

racial bias, 19–20
racism, 37
regret, 105
Reiki, 107
religious and faith-based practices, 41, 55–56, 81, 143. *See also* spiritual freedom; Spiritual Well
resilience, 121–123, 151
ritual, definition of, 160
rituals and routines, 159–172
 annual ritual, 165–171
 daily practice to center and honor yourself, 171–172
 daily ritual, 163–164
 daily routine, 161–163
 3Ps ritual, 164–165
routine, definition of, 160
routines. *See* rituals and routines

sandwich generation, 5
Saxena, Silvi, 47
segregation, 19–20
self-care, 74, 102, 120–124
self-compassion, 111, 137
self-doubt, 25, 96, 138
selfishness, 117–124, 129–130
self-sacrifice, 10, 25, 112, 119–120, 129, 175

self-talk, 5
shame, 104–105
slavery and slave trade, 9, 58, 108–109
social freedom, 144
social media, 21, 31, 88, 102, 151
Social Well, 42, 54–55, 57, 80, 96. *See also* Personal Wells
solitude, 87–90, 91, 98, 159
spiritual freedom, 142–143
Spiritual Well, 42, 55–56, 57, 81, 96–97. *See also* Personal Wells
Stic (stic.man), 125, 127
strangers, 2, 3, 114, 127, 170, 173
sunsets, 3–4

television, 28, 29, 31, 92
TERMS (time, energy, relationships, money, sanity), 128–130, 135, 150, 155, 159, 160
terms, setting your, 124–131
3Ps ritual, 164–165
time freedom, 145
toxic positivity, 20
trauma, 30, 99
Tubajon, Robbie, 125–126

unwell, state of being, 32–42, 49, 50, 91
  definition of, 40
  freedom and, 76, 156
  overwhelm and, 9–11, 48
  resilience and, 123
  rumination and, 83

vacations, 1–4, 21, 98
vulnerability, 98, 137

wellness. *See* health and wellness; Personal Wells; unwell, state of being
Wells. *See* Personal Wells
Wilson, Tieko Nejon, 22–23

YOUR NOTES

ABOUT THE AUTHOR

Christine Platt is an advocate for embracing the power of less to simplify, surrender, and boldly step into the next season of life. Author of *The Afrominimalist's Guide to Living with Less*, she holds a BA in Africana Studies from the University of South Florida, MA in African and African American Studies from The Ohio State University, and JD from Stetson University College of Law. Now an empty nester, Christine lives her best intentional life with less in Washington, DC, and Marrakech, Morocco.